LOST WORLDS AND MYSTERIOUS CIVILIZATIONS

Easter Island

LOST WORLDS AND MYSTERIOUS CIVILIZATIONS

Atlantis

Easter Island

El Dorado

The Maya

Nubia

Pompeii

Roanoke

Troy

Contents

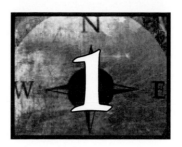

Polynesian Wayfinders

Perhaps as many as a thousand years before Christopher Columbus left the safety and familiarity of continental Europe to venture west, out across the uncharted Atlantic, the Polynesian king Hotu Matu'a (Great Parent), along with 200 to 300 men, women, and children, sailed east into the vast openness of the eastern Pacific. Unlike Columbus, however, Hotu Matu'a was on a voyage of discovery, exploration, and, significantly, colonization. Having been defeated in battle and, as a consequence, exiled in search of an unknown land, the king had little choice in taking to the sea.

According to legend, after launching two 90-foot-long, 6-foot-deep (27-meters-long, 1.8-m-deep) canoes, which may have taken three years to carve out with stone axes from giant tree trunks, the king and his voyagers set out from Hiva (in the Marquesas Islands group), with a coconut-leaf sail unfurled and paddlers straining against the ocean currents and opposing winds. Or they may have departed from Mangareva, an island a thousand miles southeast of Tahiti, in what is today French Polynesia.

The two canoes, strapped together to form a catamaran, were joined by a bridge, from which a mast arose. A small, thatched-roof shelter provided some protection from the elements. As a colonizing venture, not just one of discovery and exploration, the catamaran carried not only ample supplies for a journey of weeks, if not months, but enough flora and fauna to establish a new settlement. A 50-foot (15-m) canoe was capable of carrying upward of 18,000 pounds (8,165 kilograms), so there was no problem in storing plentiful supplies plus crew and passengers.

But the journey now to be undertaken, abundant provisions aside, was fraught with danger and uncertainty. A stout vessel, with a strong crew having a thorough understanding of marine ecology, not to mention celestial navigation, was required if the voyagers were to have any chance of finding a new place to inhabit.

Yet, Hotu Matu'a, or Polynesians like him, did miraculously succeed in chasing the rising sun for weeks on end to discover and colonize a land that is, even today, considered the most remotely, continuously inhabited place on Earth. Twenty-five-hundred miles east of Tahiti, and almost an equal distance west from mainland Chile, Easter Island, a 64-square-mile speck in the southeast Pacific, was, indeed, discovered and settled. Hotu Matu'a, upon sighting the island, was said to have first circumnavigated the triangular-shaped, cliff-hanging volcanic haven three times, then, seeing a small beach, landed his founding party at what is today Anakena.

Hotu Matu'a and his weary voyagers, upon arriving on Easter Island (also known as Rapa Nui), found a subtropical refuge but no tropical paradise. At the time, though the island was blessed with tall palm trees, of which there may have been as many as 16 million, there were no mammals or fruit-bearing trees and no protective reefs. Luckily, the voyagers came prepared, with the tools, food, plants, and animals they needed to begin a new life, one in which their descendants for 25 to 50 generations hence were destined to live out in complete isolation—cut off from all other human contact.

MIGRATORY ADVANCEMENT

The Polynesians' ever eastward, island-grabbing infusion into the Pacific, culminating in the settlement of distant Easter Island, would turn out to be the last leg of a human migration that began 50,000 years ago, the origins of which can be traced to the heart of East Africa, a half a world away. Beginning much earlier with *Homo erectus*, to be followed by *Homo heidelbergensis*, then *Homo neanderthalensis*, our predecessors migrated north, out of Africa, into Europe, through Asia, to as far as the island of Borneo, part of present-day Malaysia and Indonesia. All three of these early groups died out, however. With *Homo sapiens* (modern humans), the migrations were even more far flung, and, of course, more successful, since the species survives today to, among other things, read this book.

Early Polynesians living in the Pacific used canoes to hunt, travel, and colonize other islands in the region. An exiled Polynesian king and a small group of his followers were possibly the first to inhabit Easter Island, a small piece of land located between Tahiti and Chile.

About 40,000 years ago, our ancestors reached into China, down through Southeast Asia, and onto the Australian continent.

The last great ice age of 40,000 to 60,000 years ago, which locked up in glaciers millions of cubic miles of precipitation that would normally have gone into the oceans, dropped the level of the sea as much as 300 feet. As a consequence, migration across numerous land bridges joining most of Southeast Asia, as well as New Guinea, Australia, and Tasmania, became feasible. *Homo sapiens* moved ever eastward.

The majority could walk to their new homes. Significantly, however, a few innovators developed some sort of maritime technology, which allowed them to travel and explore offshore. "By 40,000 years ago they had reached islands that stretched, chain-like, from New Guinea's south-east coast—New Britain and New Ireland," wrote K.R. Howe, in *Vaka Moana: Voyages of the Ancestors*. "Although these islands were in sight of each other, there were others far beyond the horizon that were, nevertheless, still reached. Buka, in the Solomon Islands, was settled 30,000 years ago and Manus Island some 13,000 years ago."

By 4000 B.C., when, as a result of the ice age's end the seas had risen to their present level, humans were occupying most of Southeast Asia, parts of Australia, and out to sea as far as the Solomons. They had successfully settled what is today called Near Oceania. They had yet to penetrate further eastward, however, into the vastness of Remote Oceania.

Moving on to discover, explore, and colonize the distant islands of the Pacific, following the rising sun in what many today consider the last great human terrestrial migration, would not be easy, of course. An entirely new technology and way of life, one capable of long-range ocean voyaging, along with a system of reliable navigation, would be required. Given that the islands to be encountered would often lack adequate plants and animals capable of sustaining human populations, the exploring and founding peoples would need to be more than merely hunters and gatherers, but, importantly, horticulturists as well. Daunting obstacles aside, such colonization did take place. And the humans, Polynesians to be specific, that eventually undertook settlement as far east as Easter Island, would, in so doing, complete the final chapter of human migratory progress, reaching the end of the habitable world.

BOAT PEOPLE EXTRAORDINAIRE

The first watercraft to be used by those willing to venture off their coasts, mainly to fish, were undoubtedly rafts made of bamboo or logs tied together. Such rafts were passable for drifting and steering with the current. They were, however, hard to paddle. If equipped with a sail, they could proceed with the wind, but, importantly, not against it. Though a good start on the way to seafaring, the rafts used by early inhabitants of Near Oceania were almost never employed to seek out unseen lands over the horizon.

The single dugout canoe, hollowed out from a large tree trunk, offered a considerable advantage over the raft. It had more buoyancy, and paddling was much easier. However, such a canoe had one major drawback—with a rounded cross section, it was easily capsized.

With the invention of the outrigger, either single or double, much greater stability was obtained, and when such a canoe was put to sail, great distances could be traversed. "Outriggers attached to hulls by booms provide roll stability," noted Geoffrey Irwin, professor of archaeology at the University of Auckland, in New Zealand. "When outriggers are lifted from the water their weight provides a righting movement to rotate them back to the surface; and when the rotation of the canoe hull pushes down into the water their buoyancy restores them to the surface."

From the outrigger it was a small step, but a most consequential one, to the double canoe, where two independent hulls are lashed together. "The main advantage of double canoes is their greater capacity for transporting migrants to distant lands, such as those of Eastern Polynesia," wrote Ben Finney, professor of anthropology at the University of Hawaii. "Double canoes and double outriggers also avoid the problems inherent in tacking single-outrigger canoes, as their opposing hulls or floats serve, depending on the wind direction, alternatively as balancing weights and pontoons to keep the craft stable."

When coupled with an effective sail, a double canoe, of the type Hotu Matu'a may have used in voyaging east to find a new home, could be quite effective for the long, arduous journey ahead. Dr. Jo Anne Van Tilburg, in her book *Among Stone Giants*, summarized what the evolved sailing technology meant for Polynesians, as explorers and colonizers, at the time of Easter Island's discovery. "On islands possessing large hardwood trees, sailing vessels evolved into double-hulled, double-masted canoes from forty-nine to seventy-two feet long," the archaeologist stated. "Their masts, sails, and steering paddles were proportionately huge. A living platform straddled the two hulls, a community of people lived aboard it in the same manner they had lived in their land-based villages, and each person had his or her place and task."

Building and launching such double canoes during the first millennium A.D. was a momentous achievement, especially for a stone-age people, carving away with rocks, bones, and coral. Of equal or even greater accomplishment, however, was the Polynesians' incredible ability to find their way among the vast watery emptiness all around them, to, in other words, understand how to navigate their vessels.

STAR NAVIGATORS

"A seaman who intends more than a local passage, who proposes to sail to a destination which he cannot see from his point of departure, needs, in addition to a reliable vessel, a means of finding his way," wrote John H. Parry, in *The Discovers of the Sea*. In most cases, that Polynesian seaman was both a man of chiefly rank and the vessel's navigator. He had absolute power aboard his voyaging canoe and was prepared, at all times, to make life or death decisions. According to Van Tilburg, in her book *Easter Island: Archaeology, Ecology, and Culture*, "Navigation was a highly specialized science, taught to high-ranking and/or highly gifted men in organized and secret schools of learning. The power of the navigator was derived from the gods and was made visible in profound and striking ways, time and again, throughout the journey."

To seek land out of sight, what is known as "wayfinding," Polynesian navigators needed to orient themselves and know how to home in on a target island before it could be seen. Being able to do so often involved a lifetime of learning, along with more than a little bit of luck.

The navigator's challenge was, first and foremost, to use the stars and other celestial bodies for course setting and steering. Joseph Banks, an eighteenth-century sailor on the *Endeavor*, prowling the South Pacific, noted how acquainted with the stars the Polynesians were:

> *Of these they know a very large part by their names and the clever ones among them will tell in what part of the heavens they are to be seen in any month when they are above the horizon; they also know the time of their annual appearing and disappearing to a great nicety, far greater than would be easily believed by a European astronomer.*

To zero in on an island, to find land before it was visible, oceanic navigators used several clever and intriguing approaches. According to Ben Finney, writing in *Vaka Moana*:

> *These [methods] included looking for land nesting birds that daily fish out to sea at a limited distance from their island, watching for trade wind clouds piling up above an island that is still below the horizon, looking for green reflections of shallow atoll lagoons projected onto the undersides of clouds, detecting characteristic disruptions in the ocean swells caused by islands, and observing streaks of phosphorescence in the sea that point toward islands. Technically, these methods can be called piloting techniques in that they are ways of remotely sensing land.*

It is critical to point out that in locating an island, one that may be but a few miles in width, pinpoint accuracy was not required. "A radius of 50 to 75 miles around an island brings one within the area where birds, winds, land-clouds, and the altered swell patterns of the ocean can be used as guides," wrote John Flenley and Paul Bahn, in *The Enigmas of Easter Island*. "By 'expanding' the difficult targets in this way, it was possible simply to steer for entire archipelagos, and then use the 'radius phenomena' as one approached."

Flenley and Bahn go on to note that even tiny Easter Island would be extended tenfold by using the indicators listed above. Hotu Matu'a had his methods, no doubt about it.

WITH FULL INTENT

But why go at all? Why would Polynesian seafarers choose to leave the island homes they knew so well to venture east in search of lands that they had no assurances they would ever find? "The history of settlement and cultural development of the Pacific region is one of the most dramatic chapters of the recent history of mankind," wrote Andreas Mieth and Hans-Rudolf Bork, in their book, *Easter Island—Rapa Nui: Scientific Pathways to Secrets of the Past*. "Overcoming the enormous distances between the islands and atolls of the Pacific called for nautical and logistical skills never attained by other peoples and hardly comprehensible today. The conquest of the so-called 'Polynesian Triangle,' the central Pacific region between New Zealand, Hawaii, and Easter Island, was a matter of a mere 1,200 years."

Natural catastrophes affecting already settled regions (that is, earthquakes, volcanic eruptions, floods, and typhoons) may have driven some to seek refuge elsewhere. Overpopulation could have been a factor, with islands already occupied eventually reaching the limits of human sustainability.

Trade must have been a compelling factor in many cases. "Occupants of some Polynesian islands are known to have gone very considerable distances looking for raw materials or suitable types of stone for tool-making or tomb-building," noted Flenley and Bahn. Wars could have been a factor, with resulting exile the only way out for defeated populations. A related aspect may have been the desire of younger, junior chiefs

When explorers stumbled upon Easter Island, they discovered the moai—large, upright statues carved out of stone. The significance of the moai and how they were created, moved, and erected mystified scholars and drew many visitors to the island.

to establish new lines of descent on "virgin" islands. And not to be discounted is the issue of human curiosity, adventure, or simply wanderlust.

Central to the question as to why Polynesians continued to move east, occupying island after island, out into the vast Pacific, even when such islands became fewer and farther apart, is the matter of "accident or competence." In other words, did Polynesian sailors, or fishermen, simply drift off course while out at sea and, by accident, "find" new lands? Or did they go forth on purpose, with full deliberation and intent, on voyages, though perilous and, more often than not, defeating, of not only discovery but colonization?

The scholarly evidence to date is clear on this matter—Polynesians knew what they were doing when they set out on oceanic voyages, and they sought new islands on purpose. "The fact that animals and plants were always transported to the new settlements argues strongly against the colonization being accidental," noted Flenley and Bahn. "Would offshore fishermen, unexpectedly caught by a storm, happen to have not only their womenfolk but also dogs, chickens, pigs, and rats on board as well as banana sprouts and a wide range of other useful plants? The transporting of complete 'landscapes' to new islands suggests organized colonizing expeditions."

While Hotu Matu'a did not know exactly where he was going, he did set forth with planning and intent.

For the next 1,500 years, the island Hotu Matu'a, or Polynesian voyagers like him, settled would come to mystify and intrigue all who encountered it. Chief among the enigmas that draw thousands to Easter Island every year are the moai, giant stone statues, nearly a thousand of which exist in various stages of construction. Why these edifices were created and how they were carved, transported, and erected, and why they were eventually torn down are issues that, for the most part, no longer baffle scholars. There is, however, much about Easter Island that still does.

Learning how Hotu Matu'a's descendants coped with the unprecedented challenges they faced, some of which still exist today, may well be a discovery worthy of the initial effort the king, himself, undertook.

The Center
of the World

Easter Island is located at one of three apexes that form what is known as the Polynesian Triangle. In the north is Hawaii; at the southeast, New Zealand; and on the far eastern end, Easter Island. Each leg of the triangle is 7,000 miles (11,265 kilometers) long. The island is 2,300 miles (3,701 km) west of South America and 2,500 miles (4,023 km) east of Tahiti. It is 3,700 miles (5,955 km) north of Antarctica. The closest inhabited island is tiny Pitcairn, 1,260 miles (2,028 km) to the west, where the mutineers of the H.M.S. *Bounty* settled in 1790. Easter Island is one remote, isolated place.

The 64-square mile (166-square kilometer) speck that is, today, Easter Island was formed by the eruption of three major hot spot volcanoes. The Pacific Ocean floor has many fissures that mark the limits between various tectonic plates. At these points, magma, or liquid rock, constantly emerges and then solidifies to regenerate Earth's surface. At some places, these fissures in the ocean floor result in hot spots, which produce volcanoes. The tops of these volcanoes will now and then climb high enough to form Pacific Islands.

The first volcano that would eventually create Easter Island, known as Poike, erupted approximately 3 million years ago, forming a conical peninsula that is, today, 1,217 feet (370 m) above sea level but extends 11,400 feet (3,474 m) down to the seafloor. Its crater, known as Pua Katiki, is dry, 500 feet (152 m) in diameter, and between 33 and 50 feet (10 and 15 m) deep.

The volcano Rano Kau was the second to erupt, approximately 2 million years before the present. It is close to 1,000 feet (305 m) above the sea, with a huge caldera two-thirds of a mile across. The cavity is filled with a

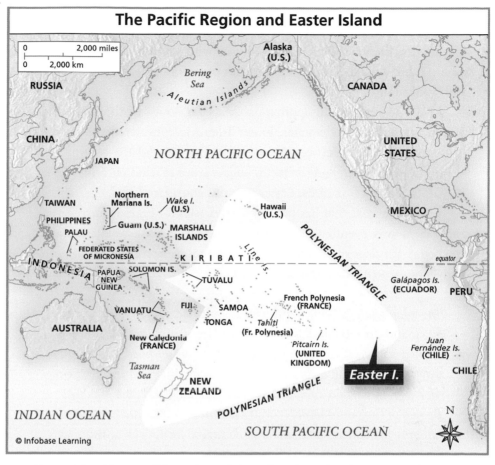

The Pacific Region and Easter Island

Easter Island is one of the points of the Polynesian Triangle, a region that encompasses more than 1,000 islands in the Pacific Ocean. Polynesians traveled by canoe to different islands throughout the triangle, which includes New Zealand, Samoa, Tahiti, and Hawaii.

freshwater bog 36 feet (11 m) deep. Rano Kau is, without a doubt, one of the most impressive, awe-inspiring geological sites on the planet.

Terevaka, the youngest of the three volcanoes to configure Easter Island, spouted forth close to 300,000 years ago. Rano Aroi is its main crater, 657 feet (200 m) in diameter, with a small lagoon. Terevaka rises to 1,680 feet (512 m), the highest point on the island.

The triangular-shaped land that is Easter Island is a result of these three volcanoes erupting and, through a slow, natural eroding process, "coming together." Easter Island's topography is mostly gentle, with deep valleys and numerous hills. Small coral formations exist along the shore-line, but the lack of a coral reef means that the sea has cut cliffs around much of the island. The coastline is infused with numerous caves and lava tubes. There are only two sandy beaches on the northeast coast: Ovahe and Anakena.

At 27 degrees south, approximately as far south of the equator as Miami is north of the equator, Easter Island is considered subtropical, with a mild climate. Between 30 and 61 inches (76 and 155 centimeters) of rain fall each year, and the mean temperature reaches 69°F (21°C). By Polynesian Island standards, Easter Island is considered cool.

While the land that has become Easter Island began as barren rock and ash, it was eventually colonized by seabirds. As a result, it slowly greened, with deposits of plant seeds and guano. According to Jo Anne Van Tilburg, writing in *Among Stone Giants*:

> *The island has an embarrassment of volcanic stone riches: dense, hard, and dark basalt; black volcanic glass; and porous tuffs, some stained and deep, rich red of oxidized iron. Sunset-hued clouds give way to a glistening nighttime canopy of stars, then return through morning mists and rainbows to cast scudding daytime shadows. Rooted in cool, unbelievably turquoise waters more than a thousand fathoms [6,000 feet] deep, the island's ragged and rocky coastline is punctuated with a few small landing spots, a pink-sand cove, and one large beach.*

For Hotu Matu'a and his colonizing party, "Te Pito Te Henua," or "the navel of the world" (the center of everything), must have seemed a most inviting place indeed.

THERE TO STAY

The island that Hotu Matu'a found 1,000 to 1,500 years ago differed, how-ever, in one critical respect from the island of today. Upon arrival, the king surveyed a land crowded with trees, a dense forest of large palms (perhaps as many as 16 million) covering 70 percent of Easter Island. The existence of such vast woodlands would turn out to have major consequences for Hotu Matu'a's descendants. In turn, the eventual total decimation of the forest would have even greater significance for the island population.

Three separate volcanic eruptions resulted in the formation of Easter Island. The crater of Rano Kau, the second volcano that erupted approximately 2 million years ago, is still visible and is filled with a freshwater bog.

But with that day of reckoning still a way off, at the moment of settlement, Hotu Matu'a's first task was to examine the local flora and fauna in order to understand quickly what could provide sustenance. Because of the thick forests, generous precipitation resulted. As a consequence, early islanders were blessed with freshwater from perennial streams and from the three crater swamps of Rano Aroi, Rano Kau, and Rano Raraku (*rano* means crater lake). In addition, water pools often collected in the island's countless lava tubes. The initial settlers would not die of thirst.

Nor would they starve. For starters, seabirds and land birds existed in the millions. The Rapanui (islanders) ate sooty terns, storm petrels, fulmars, albatross, boobies, rails, shearwaters, doves, herons, barn owls, and parrots. And, of course, they consumed the virtually unlimited supply of eggs, a protein source that would take centuries to exhaust. Birds, particularly seabirds, also provided a valuable assist in that they indicated the location of shoals of edible fish.

Of the 167 varied creatures found in the waters off Easter Island, the common dolphin, a porpoise, was the most sought after. This, the largest animal available to the islanders, was, as time progressed, harpooned far offshore in large canoes built from the abundant palms of the island. Small shellfish were also gathered and eaten, usually raw, and crayfish and crabs were a delicacy often sought after. In addition, turtles, seals, and, significantly, tuna were available.

Of course, Hotu Matu'a brought with him plants and animals he hoped would flourish on the new landfall. Referring to settlement of the

RATS AND DEFORESTATION

If, upon arrival sometime between A.D. 700 and 1000, Hotu Matu'a, or voyagers like him, surveyed an island with as many as 16 million palm trees, how is it that they were all gone by the time Westerners arrived in the eighteenth century? What caused the massive deforestation? Clearly, humans were the main culprits, chopping down, stone thrust by stone thrust, trees to be used for building canoes, transporting and erecting moai, building fires, making carvings, constructing houses, and so forth. That said, deforestation may have been given a helping hand from an unlikely, though at times a welcomed source—the Polynesian rat, *Rattus exulans*.

Of course, Polynesian rats, most likely introduced at settlement, by accident or on purpose, did not actually gnaw away at palm tree trunks, cutting the trees down with their tiny teeth. What they did, it is claimed, was eat the trees' nuts, thus preventing propagation. In other words, humans cut the trees down, and rats prevented new ones from germinating. Both factors resulted in deforestation.

John Flenley and Paul Bahn, in their book, *The Enigmas of Easter Island*, make the following case for rats having contributed to Easter Island deforestation:

Polynesian Triangle in general, Catherine and Michel Orliac, writing in *Easter Island: Mystery of the Stone Giants*, declared: "These sea peoples brought the plants necessary for their food, care, and clothes, along with certain trees needed for their utilitarian and symbolic functions. The taro, the yam, the sweet potato, and the banana were thus introduced to the new lands."

Of the animals carried to Easter Island at settlement, the dog seems not to have survived. The chicken, however, did and multiplied to become a valuable food source. So, too, did an intentional or unintentional "guest," the Polynesian rat, *Rattus exulans*, the third most widespread species of its kind in the world. While the wily rodent, with its large round ears,

"Why then, did the palm become extinct?" the authors ask.

One answer lies in tooth marks: every Paschalococos nut so far recovered, apart from the fragments from Anakena, had been gnawed by rodents, . . . Some of the gnawed nuts found on Easter Island were submitted by Flenley to Dr. A.J. Stuart of Cambridge University, a specialist on Britain's Quaternary mammals, in the hope that he would pronounce them the product of rat's teeth. He did not. He said the tooth marks were more the size that would be produced by the teeth of mice. This was disturbing, for mice are not abundant on Easter Island. It then transpired, however, that the archaeological dig at Anakena had turned up numerous remains of the Polynesian rat, Rattus exulans. The island's present rat, Rattus rattus, had been introduced only after European contact, when it had rapidly ousted the Polynesian rat.

Rattus exulans, it turns out, is a very small, mouse-sized species. Now Dr. Stuart's findings fit. Clearly, the nuts found in the caves were gnawed by Rattus exulans, which was probably the only rodent on the island at the time.

pointed snout, black/brown hair, and tiny feet would prove to be a useful source of protein, the negative consequences of its introduction would be profound. It is now extinct on the island, although its "brother," the European rat, is, unfortunately, abundant.

For Hotu Matu'a and his colonizers, along with their descendants for generations to come, Easter Island was now home. The island did have its means—enough to allow for a significant population expansion as the centuries wore on. That was all to the good, for what would later be called the Rapanui, were, like it or not, on Easter Island to stay. They were, in effect, isolated, living at the farthest stretch of Remote Oceania.

AGRICULTURAL RESOURCES

The Chilean wine palm (*Jubaea chilensis*) is today the largest palm tree in the world. The palm Hotu Matu'a and his colonizers found on Easter Island in such abundance (*Jubaea sp.*) was clearly related to the mainland variety. The Easter Island tree was even larger than the Chilean wine palm, however, often reaching a height of 65 feet (20 m) and a diameter of 7 feet (2 m). It was the biggest palm tree ever to have existed.

According to Jared Diamond, writing in his book *Collapse*:

> *Chileans prize their palm today for several reasons and Easter Islanders would have done so as well. As the name implies, the trunk yields a sweet sap that can be fermented to make wine or boiled down to make honey or sugar. The nuts' oily kernels are rated a delicacy. The fronds are ideal for fabricating into house thatching, baskets, mats, and boat sails. And, of course, the stout trunks would have served to transport and erect Moai [stone statues], and perhaps make rafts.*

Indeed, the early settlers of Easter Island made extensive use of the island-wide palm trees they found all around them. Initially, the palm forests were used for crop production. Various vegetables and fruits were planted in between the palm trees, the latter offering protection for the smaller plants. According to Andreas Mieth and Hans-Rudolf Bork, in *Easter Island—Rapa Nui*, "It [the palm tree] gave them [the crops] shade and protected them against transpiration and wind. The forest vegetation also protected the soil, as the canopy of the trees kept direct impact of rain and wind away and thus prevented soil erosion. The garden soils were sustainably enriched with organic substance by mulching of plant remains."

Eventually, settlers took horticulture in the palm forests one significant step further by applying widespread slash-and-burn methods. "The palms were chopped off with stone tools only a few centimeters above the soil surface and the leaves and other useless parts were probably removed at the place of felling," report Mieth and Bork. "The trunks were then taken out and put to various uses. The remains of the palms, their stumps, the litter—including some fallen-down nuts—as well as the waste from other non-usable plants were burned."

Among the crops grown in and around the palm forests of Easter Island after settlement was the *Ipomoea batatas*, or sweet potato, a plant whose existence on the island has plagued Pacific and New World researchers for decades. Botanists agree that the sweet potato originated in South America. Its seeds, however, cannot survive direct saltwater voyaging. Therefore, the only plausible way the plant could have made it to Easter Island was by human transport. The sweet potato was probably introduced into central Polynesia from South America before A.D. 700. It was then, in turn, brought to Easter Island by Polynesians at settlement, and thus, according to Van Tilburg, "the transfer was made by Polynesians after a voyage of exploration to the South American coast." It is an intriguing possibility that Polynesians actually reached South America, returned with the sweet potato to central Polynesia, and then, as they sailed eastward to Easter Island, brought the plant with them.

Thus as the first Easter Islanders settled in, they made extensive use of not only the flora found native to the island, such as the palm tree, but what plant life they brought with them, in particular, the sweet potato. Consequently, as in centuries past, a Polynesian life began to flourish on a new island home.

SOCIAL ORGANIZATION

Hotu Matu'a, as legend would have it, became the first king of Easter Island. On his voyage of discovery, he had with him six sons. As Hotu Matu'a lay dying, he divided the entire island among the six. According to Van Tilburg:

Each plot of land was commensurate in value with each man's birth order within the family. The eldest inherited the greatest share of his father's mana [supernatural power], the royal estate lands of Anakena, and the powerful title of paramount chief. The youngest son, called Hotu Iti, was his father's favorite and received the entire eastern portion of the island—including Rano Raraku [the stone quarry]. This legacy acknowledged that Hotu Iti, although outranked by his brothers, was somehow gifted.

Thus, soon enough, Easter Island split into tribes, or Mata. Each one of Hotu Matu'a's six sons founded a main Mata. Each Mata, was, in turn, subdivided into Ure, or groups of families. The Mata leader was the oldest man who could trace his personal lineage directly back to one of Hotu Matu'a's sons.

The social hierarchy that would quickly develop on the island can be broken down as follows:

- At the apex was the Ariki Mau, the king and spiritual leader of the island. He possessed the most mana.
- The Ariki Paka were the aristocrats.
- Tangata Honui were important elders who advised the Ariki Mau and leaders of the Ure.
- The high priests were known as Ivi Atua.
- The Matato'a were prominent warriors of each clan.
- The Paoa were warriors of lower status than the Matato'a.
- Maori were experts in different arts and disciplines.
- And, finally, at the bottom of the hierarchy were the Kio. They could be servants, refugees, or even slaves.

In effect, Ariki Mau ruled all of Easter Island. According to Steven Roger Fischer, writing in *Island at the End of the World*:

He [the Ariki Mau] was the one individual with the most aristocratic pedigree and the most exalted social position on the island. His person was overflowing with mana and his sacredness caused him to be feared and respected. His function in society was to ensure through his very being the abundance of crops and the fertility of the ground and to exercise his influence on animal life. Certain religious

activities were derived from his sacredness and he held supervisory
control over various practices connected with religion.

For the first few centuries after discovery of the island, the Ariki Mau was seen as a living deity and as such wielded absolute power.

Eventually, the Mata of Easter Island would coalesce into two major divisions. The Ko Tu'u Aro would occupy the western side of the island, and they would be of higher social status. The Hotu Iti lived on the eastern portion of Easter Island. Their standing was of a lower rank.

Each of the six major tribes, or clans, on the island came, in time, to dominate and work a portion of the land in its own way. One group would command the most fertile part of the island, thus dedicating themselves to agriculture. Another would work the quarry at Rano Raraku, from which obsidian was obtained to create carving tools. A third clan would concentrate on the work related to the construction of canoes. Another clan would specialize in fishing. Thus, each group dedicated its energies to one specialty, with an elaborate network of trade ensuring the exchange of resources. Cooperation was the norm, and life, for the most part, was peaceful and good.

SACRED CEREMONIAL SITES

In addition to the basic supplies for survival, the original settlers of Easter Island brought with them ideas, customs, and religious practices of their central Polynesian culture. Chief among them was the construction of what would be more than 300 ahu, or stone altars—shrines. The ahu are, in many respects, an archaeological phenomenon, with some having required the moving of 300 to 500 tons of stone for their construction. The Tahai Ahu complex, for example, consists of three structures, with a total of 30,000 cubic yards of rock and earth fill, estimated to weigh 2,000 tons.

The ahu form an almost unbroken line around the coastal areas of Easter Island, with distinct clusters around coves and good landing places, areas where larger populations congregated. They are spaced, on average, about a half mile apart. According to John Flenley and Paul Bahn:

They [ahu] range in size from quite small to over 150 m (c.500 ft) in
length and up to more than 4 m (c.13 ft) in height, and comprise a
rubble core faced with masonry, for which no mortar was used. The

Early Polynesian colonizers built raised platforms or altars, called *ahu*, on Easter Island. Families used ahus as a meeting place for religious ceremonies and community events and would later place moai atop some of them.

seaward facades often seem to have been placed as close to the shore as possible and parallel to it, forming impressive walls which seem to rise straight out of the sea. These facades vary from uncut local stones to precisely carved and fitted blocks. To the landward side was a ramp, paved with lines of beach boulders and sloping down to an artificially flattened plaza.

Each ahu belonged to a family group, located on the territory where the family or clan lived. They seem to have been, in many cases, boundary markers, delineating clan territory.

The ahu were also, in a few cases, burial places, or abodes of the dead. Yet this does not seem to have been their original function. Most ahu had multiple roles, serving as social and ritual centers and as a lineage and boundary marker. According to Flenley and Bahn: "Burial seems to have been the exception rather than the rule in early periods of Rapa Nui, since no early skeletons have been found: cremation was far more common, and elaborate cremation pits have been found behind the central platform at many complexes such as Akivi or Ahu O Rongo."

In actual construction, the classic elements of an ahu are

- a retaining rear wall several feet high, usually facing the sea;
- a platform behind the wall;
- pads or cushions on the platform;
- a sloping ramp covered with evenly sized, wave-round boulders on the inland side of the platform rising most of, but not all, the way up the side of the platform;
- a pavement in front of the ramp;
- an interior filled with rubble.

In the square (an open space extending in front of the central platform), people performed community, ceremonial, and religious meetings. With some ahu there existed a circular space bordered by stones, where memorial ceremonies in honor of illustrious dead men took place.

The ahu were clearly major archaeological wonders in their own right. Even modest ahu would have taken months to construct, with, perhaps, two dozen men working full time at the task. Yet, as will be seen shortly, of the 313 known ahu, 125 would eventually gain a powerful enhancement, carrying upon their raised platforms the famous moai, large stone statues for which, above all else, Easter Island is known and venerated.

Megalithic Monuments

When Easter Island is the subject, it is an image of the island's moai, megalithic volcanic statues, that is conjured up. With nearly a thousand identified, albeit in various stages of completion, one would be hard-pressed to miss them on a 64-square mile (166-square km) landmass. It is the moai, above all, that give Easter Island its "mysterious" patina, its main reason for study, inquiry, and wonder. Just what are they? Why were they carved? How were they transported from their main quarry to the island's northern and southern coasts? How were they erected? And, finally, why were virtually all those that once stood pulled down? Thanks to exhaustive research going back over a century or more, we have informed answers to these and related questions. Having, for the most part, solved the "moai mystery," however, in no way diminishes their wonder. On the contrary, it only enhances it.

Archaeologist Jo Anne Van Tilburg, who has devoted a good portion of her professional career to studying the moai, succeeded in identifying and documenting 887 statues by the late 1980s. Of that number, 397 (45 percent) are still in situ, "resting" in their central production center, "their maternity ward," at the Rano Raraku volcano. Fully 288 statues (32 percent) were successfully transported to a variety of ahu, the latter then to become "image ahu." Another 92 (10 percent) are noted as being "in transport." And 47 (5 percent) are lying in various positions on prepared roads or tracks outside the Rano Raraku zone.

The moai are human heads on torsos, carved in the male form from rough, hardened volcanic ash. While the casual visitor might be excused in assuming they are monolithic and identical as can be carved, in actuality, each one represents an important ancestor of a given clan and is unique, if only slightly different from its fellows.

Carved, for the most part, between the eleventh and sixteenth centuries, the moai average 13.29 feet (4 m) in height, have a base width of 5.25 feet (1.6 m), a head that is 4.86 feet (1.5 m) wide, and a depth through the body at midpoint of 3.02 feet (1 m). The average volume is calculated to be 210 cubic feet (5.94 cubic meters). Total weight of the typical moai is 13.78 tons (12.5 metric tons).

While a few of the moai were carved from rock other than that found at Rano Raraku, it is from this long-extinct volcano that almost all have found their origin. Thor Heyerdahl, writing in his book *Aku-Aku*, published in 1958, gives a vivid account of Rano Raraku, when he declares:

> *Rano Raraku remains one of the greatest and most curious monuments of mankind. . . . The whole mountain massif has been reshaped, the volcano has been greedily cut up as if it were pastry, although sparks fly when a steel ax is driven against the rock to test its strength. Hundreds of thousands of cubic feet of rock have been cut out and tens of thousands of tons of stone carried away. And in the midst of the mountain's gaping wound lie more than a hundred and fifty gigantic stone men, in all stages from the just begun to the just completed. At the foot of the mountain stand finished stone men side by side like a supernatural army.*

The largest moai ever carved has been given the name "El Gigante." The statue has a length of 65 feet and is estimated to weigh 165 tons (150 metric t). It lies unfinished on the outer slope of Rano Raraku, occupying a full, almost inaccessible ridge. Anyone who has seen El Gigante close up cannot help but conclude that this moai was never intended to be moved but, rather, to remain as part of the mountain, like a Mount Rushmore figure. Today, there is not a crane in all of South America that could lift El Gigante, even if it could, somehow be cut loose from its mooring. El Giante is, in effect, an enormous petroglyph.

HONORED ANCESTORS

It is believed that the moai represented ancestors, chiefs, or other high-ranking individuals who held an important place in the history of Easter

Most moai are carved from the Rano Raraku volcano and transported to ahus located throughout the island. Thousands of tourists have traveled to Easter Island to marvel at the size and details of these unique statues.

Island. They were "living faces," the quintessential Polynesian icon, their purpose being to keep alive the memory of forebears. According to Van Tilburg, the moai were "a reassuringly familiar, straightforward and clean-lined image which was a predictable, stable, and unvarying feature of the natural/supernatural landscape for many generations. Visually, they were as a word repeated in a chant, a step repeated in a dance. It was myth made visible in support of the traditional social status quo."

The moai were made to be placed upon ahu. In time, 125 image ahu came to be, with the moai having their backs to the sea, the still-powerful ancestors facing their respective villages as protectors. The moai, along with the ahu they stood upon, represented the prolongation of earthly power and contact with the heavens. "These towering vertical figures on their horizontal platforms around the coast served as a sacred border between two worlds, as intermediaries between the living and the gods, between life and death," wrote Van Tilburg. "Transitional areas of this kind tend to be of significance in all human societies."

As time went on, the moai seem to have gotten bigger and more elaborate. Clearly, a competition was under way, where independent kin groups from different parts of the island vied to outdo their neighbors in producing ever grander statues. This prestige game manifested itself whereby some groups poured all their resources into the creation of one giant figure, such as one called Paro. In other cases, it was the number of moai placed on a given ahu that enhanced a clan's stature. At Tongariki, 15 statues were erected on a single platform. And at Anakena, the rivalry manifested itself with moai carved in distinctive, elaborate designs. More and better moai demonstrated the power and organizational capacity of a given clan.

Construction of the moai was clearly a group labor, "a volunteer effort performed for the promise of supernatural returns; rather like the medieval cathedral builder of Europe," noted Steven Roger Fischer. "Major subsistence projects in other prehistoric Polynesian societies, such as stone aqueducts, great fishponds, huge taro terraces, and breadfruit pits were missing on Easter Island. Here, all effort went into ever more impressive *ahu* and *Moai*"

That said, at least one writer, though by his own admission, no scholar, has claimed that none of the moai were really carved and transported by Easter Islanders at all. According to Swiss pulp nonfiction author Erich Von Däniken, in his famous (if not infamous) book *Return to the Stars*, published in 1972, a follow-up to his even more popular and questionable *Chariots of the Gods* (1968), construction of the moai could only have been accomplished by extraterrestrials! To Von Däniken, it was all done by "ancient astronauts":

> *The men who could execute such perfect work must have possessed ultra-modern tools. . . . A small group of intelligent beings was stranded on Easter Island owing to a "technical hitch." The stranded group had a great store of knowledge, very advanced weapons and a method of working stone unknown to us. . . . Perhaps to leave the natives a lasting memory of their stay, but perhaps also as a sign to the friends who were looking for them, the strangers extracted a colossal statue from the volcanic stone.*

In addition to being pure nonsense, Von Däniken's assertions can be interpreted as being based on a condescending, patronizing, if not racist, view of Easter Islanders, who, obviously for him, were just too stupid, too incapable of creating anything like the moai themselves. In reality, the Rapanui did, indeed, construct the moai, led by a highly skilled, efficient, and dedicated sculptor class.

WORKERS OF STONE

The Von Däniken thesis regarding statue carving on Easter Island, that a Paleolithic people, working only with stone tools, could never have carved, transported, and erected a large number of moai is, if nothing else, based on a gross misunderstanding of what can be achieved with simple technology—with lots of time, muscle power, and a good dose of ingenuity. It also fails to take into account that, with little else to do on an island that provided abundant crops, easily raised with minimum effort, islanders had plenty of time on their hands, and, therefore, that stone carving might well become a ruling passion.

It has been estimated that six men, working every day with *toki,* or basalt hand adzes (axes), could complete a 16-foot tuff moai in a year to 15 months. According to Flenley and Bahn: "Allowing a thousand statues on the island, and an estimated period of at least five hundred years of carving activity (from c. A.D. 1000 to 1500), based on radiocarbon dates from Norwegian excavations at the quarry [Rano Raraku], it is clear that even a small population could have achieved this number of figures."

To accomplish the chiseling, a specialized, privileged, master-craftsmen class of sculptors was employed. The guild carvers were undoubtedly relieved of all other work, with fishermen and farmers providing their food needs. Island-wide cooperation was required to make such a system work, and, at least during the image ahu period, relative peace must have prevailed on Easter Island.

Using toki, the sculptors would carve out the outline of a moai lying on its back. Obsidian, a glasslike rock that is formed when lava cools rapidly, is another tool that was surely used in sculpting. After chipping the outline of the statue's profile into the quarry wall, a niche was made around it so that sculptors from both sides could work. Hacking away in what was clearly a cramped space (often barely 2 feet), the carvers began by detailing the head of the moai and finished with the hips. It was then

Working in the quarry located on the slope of the Rano Raraku volcano, craftsmen would begin building a new statue by carving an outline of a moai on its back. There are approximately 397 uncompleted moai on Easter Island, many of which are still located in the quarry.

that the undercutting began. According to Katherine Routledge, writing in her monumental work *The Mystery of Easter Island*: "The rock beneath was chipped away by degrees till the statue rested only on a narrow strip of stone running along the spine; those which have been left at this stage resemble precisely a boat on its keel, the back being curved in the same way as a ship's bottom. In the next stage the statue is completely detached from the rock, and chocked up by stones, looking as if an inadvertent touch would send it sliding down the hill into the plain below."

Getting the statues lowered from Rano Raraku so their backs could be finished, was the next task, one that often resulted in broken, and thus abandoned moai. Depressed runways or channels in the earth seemed to have aided in bringing the moai to the bottom. The keel could have served to maintain the statue's direction. Ropes, made from coconut and bark fiber, may have also been used in "easing" a moai down and into a prepared pit where it would be placed into a standing position.

"Not till now, with the statues standing thus, did the sculptors set to work on the unfinished back," wrote Thor Heyerdahl. "As the neck and hinder parts took shape, a belt, decorated with rings and symbols, was carved on the waist. This little belt was the only piece of clothing the naked statues wore, and with only one exception all the colossi were male figures."

It was at this point that phase one of the moai creation and erecting process was completed. By most accounts, the hardest part lay ahead—getting the moai to their ahu, in some cases up to 12 miles (19 km) from the quarry, and then erecting them on a platform, with their backs to the sea.

DRAG AND ROLL

How the moai were transported to their destination ahu has intrigued investigators even more, perhaps, than how they were carved. Island lore has it that the statues actually "walked" to the platforms where they would be erected. Under the influence of mana (supernatural power), the moai, it has been claimed, moved to distant sites. It was said that the moai walked a short interval each day toward their ahu.

On his expedition to Easter Island in the mid-1950s, Thor Heyerdahl had an interesting conversation with the island's mayor:

> "'Don Pedro, Mayor,' I said, 'now perhaps you can tell me how your ancestors moved the figures round about on the island.'
>
> 'They went by themselves, they walked,' the mayor replied glibly.
>
> 'Rubbish,' I said, disappointed and slightly irritated.
>
> 'Take it easy! I believe that they walked, and we must respect our forefathers who have said that they walked.'"

This observation aside, the mayor does go on to tell Heyerdahl that his ancestors may well have used another method, one he called *miro manga erua*. When asked to explain what that meant, Don Pedro became more of a realist. He drew on the ground a Y-shaped figure with crosspieces and proceeded to explain that it was a sledge made from a forked tree trunk.

Indeed, most investigators, including Heyerdahl himself, believe that the moai were literally pulled from quarry to ahu, using a combination of sledge, rollers, and ropes to accomplish the task. According to Van Tilburg, Polynesian cultures in general moved large stone objects in a similar way, using a technique that would be consistent with what was needed to accomplish the movement of Easter Island moai. "In all cases, the preferred method of transport (with only minor variations) was to place the stone in a horizontal position, attach it to a wood sledge and then haul it over rollers and/or sleepers by workers pulling on ropes made of vegetable materials."

OBSIDIAN—ANCIENT CUTTING TOOL

Easter Island, having been shaped by three erupting volcanoes is, as can be expected, rich in obsidian, a naturally occurring volcanic glass formed as an extrusive igneous rock. The Rapanui used obsidian as a cutting tool, mainly to carve their moai. Fortunately, there was plenty of it to be had.

According to the Volcano World Web Site, "Obsidian is a very shiny natural volcanic glass. When obsidian breaks, it fractures with a distinct conchoidal fracture. Obsidian is produced when lava cools very quickly. The lava cools so quickly that no crystals can form. When people make glass, they melt silica rocks like sand and quartz then cool it rapidly by placing it in water. Obsidian is produced in nature in a similar way."

Ancient peoples have used obsidian as a cutting tool for weapons and for ceremonial purposes. One observer has pointed out that the making of arrowheads, spear points, knife blades, and scrapers from obsidian might have been the world's first "manufacturing industry."

The first use of obsidian probably occurred when a sharp edge on a broken piece of obsidian was used as a cutting tool. When people then discovered that obsidian could be intentionally broken to produce a cutting instrument with a variety of shapes, the "mining" of the rock began.

Lest one think that using rock as a cutting tool is "oh so prehistoric," obsidian actually continues to be used today—in modern surgery. According to geology.com, "Obsidian can be used to produce a cutting edge that is thinner and sharper than the best surgical steel. Today, thin blades of obsidian are placed in surgical scalpels used for some of the most precise surgery. In controlled studies, the performance of obsidian blades was equal to or superior to the performance of surgical steel."

Obsidian—still "cutting edge."

As Flenley and Bahn, in their study of moai transport technology, are quick to note, it was not so much the moai's weight that was a problem, but its fragility. The Rano Raraku tuff is not very dense. The key was to transport the moai without damaging the elaborate detail already carved on the figure. Clearly, with protection in mind, the moai could not have been simply drawn along the ground.

The use of a sledge placed on roller tracks, therefore, seems to have been the method of choice in moving a moai from the quarry to its waiting ahu.

The Easter Island palm, along with the endemic toromiro tree, would have worked well for the construction of both sledge and rollers. In one varied possibility, suggested by archaeologist William Mulloy, a statue would rest, facedown, on a curved Y-shaped sledge made from the fork of a big tree. "A large pair of shearlegs is attached to the figure's neck by a loop, and as they are tilted forward, the rope partially lifts the statue and takes some weight off the sledge. The statue therefore follows the shearlegs, in a kind of rocking movement caused by the bulging abdomen."

Sledge transport could have been made even more efficient—reducing the required workforce by as much as a third—by applying lubricants to the track, such as sweet potato, totora reeds, taro, yams, or palm fronds.

During his stay on Easter Island, Thor Heyerdahl, in an interesting experiment, organized a group of about 180 islanders to pull a 13-foot moai fastened to a wooden sledge. They easily moved the statue a short distance.

We do not know for sure exactly how the moai were transported. It is certainly possible, if not probable, that during the five-hundred-year period in which these amazing megalithic monuments were moved about on Easter Island, a variety of methods were used. Once having arrived at the islanders' ahu of choice, however, a moai still had to be placed upon its platform, a task requiring added engineering know-how and skill.

HEAVE-HO

Not all ahu were constructed to accept a moai. Those that would, however, had to be strengthened considerably to take the weight of one or more statues. According to Jared Diamond, Easter Islanders were only too willing to tell Thor Heyerdahl how their ancestors had erected the moai on ahu. They were upset that, for the most part, archaeologists did not deign

Featuring a head on top of a torso, each moai is a representation of a past family member or ancestor in a kin group. Although they may look the same, all moai have details that make them slightly different from one another.

to ask them how it was done. In response, the islanders raised a statue for Heyerdahl, without the use of a crane.

As Diamond explains it, "The islanders began by building a gently sloping ramp of stone from the plaza up to the top of the front of the platform, and pulling the prone statue with its base end forward up the ramp. Once the base had reached the platform, they levered the statue's head an inch or two upwards with logs, slipped stones under the head to support it in the new position, and continued to lever up the head and thereby to tilt the statue increasingly towards the vertical."

Not surprisingly, the most dangerous part of the positioning operation was the final tilting of the moai from its steep angle to the vertical position. The big fear was that the statue's momentum, in that final tilt, might simply carry it beyond the vertical and tip the whole thing off the rear of the platform. Cleverly, to reduce this risk of destroying what had been so painstakingly carved and transported up until now, the carvers designed the moai so that it was not exactly perpendicular to its flat base. Just short of perpendicular (87 degrees to the base, rather than 90 degrees), the statue's body when raised to a stable position, would still be leaning slightly forward and, as a consequence, at no major risk of tipping over backward. The moai was then, ever so slowly and carefully, levered up at the front edge of the base the final 3 degrees, using stones, until the body was vertical.

Some moai, when brought to their ahu, were crowned with a "top hat," a *pukao* headpiece made of red slag (a type of volcanic stone) found at the Paunapau volcano. Such pukao could weigh up to 11 tons (10 metric t). The pukao are believed to represent the hairstyle of the nobility, whose long hair, dyed red, was gathered into a bun on the top of the head. The pukao was probably raised, one end at a time, on scaffold that was, step-by-step, increased in height. According to Van Tilburg, a team of about 10 men using levers and the guidance of experts would have been required.

The carving, transporting, and erecting of the many moai on Easter Island between the eleventh and sixteenth centuries became central to Rapanui culture, its very reason to exist, so to speak. Yet, soon enough, the moai, to a man, were torn from their ahu, smashed to the ground. A major societal rupture had clearly occurred.

Collapse

The earliest known moai figure that originally stood upon an ahu dates from the twelfth century. The latest year for an ahu with a statue is about A.D. 1650. The so-called "golden age" of moai construction, when work became an utter obsession, was in the thirteenth century. Thus, for approximately 500 years, moai were being carved, transported, and erected on Easter Island.

During this frenzied period, the island's population increased significantly, perhaps to as many as 9,000 (one estimate puts the count as high as 15,000 by the beginning of the seventeenth century). To keep such a populated island humming, an efficient system of food exchange was needed that would, above all, feed the entire population. And this, in order to maintain a social and natural order, centered on mana-filled moai. But as Van Tilburg was quick to point out, the price islanders paid for the way they chose to articulate their spiritual and political ideas would be high. Sadly, in time the island would become but a shadow of its former natural self.

Societal underpinnings began to fall apart when overexploitation of the palm trees (in part because of their use in producing logs for the transporting and erecting of moai) manifested itself. As an outgrowth of forest depletion, the earth became more exposed, leading to serious soil erosion. Hence, fertile land that had been used for cultivation became ever scarcer. Wild food sources that everyone had been dependent on nearly vanished. According to Felipe L. Soza, writing in *Easter Island: Rapa Nui*:

As a consequence of all these things, hunger became a frequent problem
for the inhabitants of Easter Island. Also, as a result of the scarcity or
near extinction of wood supplies, the necessary resources for the con-
struction of tools and art disappeared. Without tools to build canoes,
for example, they could not go out to fish, which caused a reduction of
the food supplies normally provided by the sea. The intricate system of
exchange could not be maintained, either, due to the fact that, in order
to build Moais, it was necessary to have food surplus.

With food scarcity came famine, even starvation. The *moai kavakava*
are small wooden statuettes well known on the island. While it has not
been determined exactly when these carvings were made, ones that survive are an eerie representation of men clearly suffering from food deprivation. A typical moai kavakava depicts a man with a goatee and a hooked
nose. But his cheeks are hollow and his ribs are prominent and emaci-
ated—clear indicators of famine. The moai kavakava have a worryingly
intense gaze.

Quarrels over food may have led, logically enough, to the end of an era—
that of statue quarrying at Rano Raraku. Legend has it that an old woman
(assumed to be a witch) was denied what she felt was her rightful share of
a giant lobster. In response, the woman caused all the statue production to
cease. That said, as Flenley and Bahn more realistically point out:

It was a breakdown of the system of distribution, the exchange net-
works and the feeding of the craftsmen by the farmers and fishermen
that finally halted the group co-operation that was so vital to the
enterprise. The abandonment of work at Rano Raraku was not nec-
essarily the sudden dramatic downing of tools so beloved of the mys-
tery writers, but is more likely to have been a more gradual winding
down and disintegration of the system: in short, work quickly ground
to a halt because of an ever-increasing imbalance between the pro-
duction of essentials (food) and that of non-essentials (statues).

EATING ONE'S ENEMIES

It has been called the "divine hunger," and it is understandable that the
act is not something a culture is quick to articulate, let alone acknowledge.

Excessive moai production used up many of the island's natural resources and devastated food production and the local environment. Smaller wooden statuettes of grim, starving men were created during this time.

Cannibalism, the usually ritualistic eating of human flesh by humans, was, nonetheless, a reality, certainly in prehistoric and even early historic times. How widespread full-blown cannibalism was is open to question. Yet, the Aztec did sacrifice their prisoners of war and undoubtedly ate some of them. Fore tribal women, living in the highlands of New Guinea, who disposed of the dead, were known to have ritually eaten their deceased relatives' brains. All South Sea Islanders, it has been declared, were cannibals as far as their enemies were concerned. It turns out that when a whale ship, the *Essex*, was rammed and sunk by a whale in 1820, the captain, in a lifeboat, set sail upwind for Chile, 3,000 miles (4,828 km) away, rather than head downwind, 1,400 miles to the Marquesas, because he had heard the Marquesans were cannibals. Interestingly, many survivors of the ship-wreck resorted to cannibalism in order to survive. For whatever their reasons, the evidence seems clear that Easter Islanders, too, chose, at least at limited times, to eat human flesh.

Essentially, there are two kinds of cannibalism. There is exocannibalism, where one eats enemies, slaves, or victims captured in warfare. Endocannibalism pertains to the eating of relatives. On a simple level, exocannibalism is often a part of revenge taking, status enhancement, or the seeking of spiritual protection. The ingesting of one's victim to gain their spiritual mana was not, however, at least in Polynesia, widespread, but was limited to certain chiefs in a ritual setting.

When exocannibalism was practiced, the reprisals that followed such a crime could be monstrous. The reaction was often more violent because an act of cannibalism committed against a family member was considered the highest insult imaginable. According to Alfred Metraux, in *Easter Island—A Stone-Age Civilization of the Pacific*: "Among the Maoris [of New Zealand], those who had taken part in the meal were entitled to show their teeth to the relatives of the victim and say, 'Your flesh has stuck between my teeth.' Such remarks were capable of rousing those to whom they were addressed to a murderous rage not very different from the Malay *amok*."

Ritualistic cannibalism, it seems, did exist on Easter Island. Cannibal feasts may have taken place, where it was said that the fingers and toes were the choicest morsels. Yet, the central question regarding cannibalism on Rapanui centers on the issue of food shortages, hunger, and resulting starvation. Did the Rapanui resort to eating their fellow man in answer to prolonged hunger? As Van Tilburg noted: "Employing cannibalism as a response to hunger is not an automatic human choice, but requires the support, facilitation, and reinforcement of a cultural framework practically and ideologically congenial to the practice."

It is indeed possible, even probable, that Easter Islanders, at times in an attempt to replace their normal sources of wild meat, limited as they were, took to cannibalism as a last, cruel resource for a starving people. But to claim, as some have, that "[e]very Easter Islander knows that his ancestors were Kau Tangata, 'man-eaters,'" may be overstating the truth. A cautionary approach is warranted, and in his book, *The Complete Guide to Easter Island*, Shawn McLaughlin provides it. "It should be acknowledged that there is little or no archaeological evidence for cannibalism occurring on Easter Island, though very little research in this area has actually occurred," the author states. ". . . William Ayres reported the discovery of burned human bone fragments that suggested to him they had been 'processed' in ways that meet other criteria for cannibalism among humans, but the results are still inconclusive. Still, it's important to remember that the absence of evidence is not evidence of absence."

DEFORESTATION

How could a stone-age society destroy 16 million trees? Indeed, how could it wipe out even a million? Until recently, researchers were not even sure there had been much in the way of a forest on Easter Island. After all, when Westerners first made contact in the eighteenth century, they were quick to point out the lack of trees and the almost total absence of wood of any kind. "An island destitute of large trees," was a typical comment. "Not a single tree is to be found capable of furnishing a plank so much as six inches in width," wrote another observer. "There was not a tree upon the whole island which exceeded the height of 10 feet," it was noted. According to Flenley and Bahn, when captain Dupetit-Thouars visited the island in 1838, "Five canoes came out to his ship from the island, each carrying two men; what they most wanted was wood. Even driftwood was looked on as a treasure of inestimable value, and a dying father frequently promised to send his children a tree from the kingdom of shades."

Yet, it is John Flenley himself who is given significant credit for determining, through various techniques, that Easter Island was once covered with subtropical palm trees and then massively deforested. What happened?

And why was the deforestation of the island of such consequence for the Rapanui? Why did it lead to an almost total collapse of their society?

Although Easter Island would always lack a number of naturally available assets that humans were likely to need (large land mammals being the most obvious), nonetheless, with a forest covering upward of 70 percent of its landmass, much in the way of nourishment flowed as a consequence of tree cover. From forests came freshwater streams, and with them, animals in sufficient variety and numbers to maintain a viable society. The land was, in today's parlance, close to sustainability. Without forests, and with no outsiders to replenish resources, the Rapanui, however, would find themselves in serious trouble. A downward cycle of environmental and cultural decay would surely result.

THE FORE AND CANNIBALISM

The Fore are a group of approximately 14,000 swidden horticulturalists living in the Okapa District of the Eastern Highlands Province in Papua New Guinea. It was not until the late 1940s that outsiders established full contact with the Fore. When Australian government administrators did penetrate the Fore territorial region, it was discovered that the Fore were dying of a terrible disease, one they called *kuru*, which means "to tremble with fear." Kuru is also known as "laughing sickness," due to the outbursts of laughter that mark its second phase.

Kuru was a progressive, fatal brain malady that robbed its victims of the ability to talk, walk, and even eat. According to Rebecca Stein, writing in *The Anthropology of Religion, Magic, and Witchcraft*, "This illness [kuru] is characterized by a variety of symptoms, but the most obvious ones are jerking movements and shaking, which make planned motor activity difficult. The course of the illness is about nine months. At the end the victim can no longer stand or sit up and can no longer eat or drink water and soon dies."

At first, Australian colonial rulers thought the cause of kuru was to be found in a genetic defect, and, as a consequence, they sought

Jo Anne Van Tilburg, writing in her biography of Katherine Routledge, *Among Stone Giants*, observed that "[d]eforestation—whether it is to clear ground for planting crops, to provide fuel for cooking, to stoke the raging fires of chiefly crematoria, or to build transport rigs and lay rails to move mighty statues—leads to soil depletion, a decrease in fertility, a lessening of productivity, and a decline or permanent loss of plant species." The Easter Islander's profound creative energy on the one hand, Van Tilburg concluded, also leads to "excess that sweeps everything away to destruction."

Deforestation must have begun soon after human arrival, about A.D. 700. It would have reached its peak approximately A.D. 1400. By A.D. 1600, it was virtually complete.

---

to confine the Fore to prevent the disease from spreading. Isolation, however, did not work.

The cause of kuru, it turned out, was not a genetic defect but the social practice of cannibalism. When members of the Fore would die, others would eat the dead person, particularly the brain, during funeral rituals as a mark of respect. The corpse was dismembered, with the arms and feet removed, and the limbs stripped of muscle, the chest and head cut open, and the brain removed. According to Shirley Lindenbaum, author of *Kuru Sorcery: Disease and Danger in the New Guinea Highlands*, "Kuru victims were highly regarded as sources of food, because the layer of fat on victims who died quickly resembled pork. Women also were known to feed morsels—such as human brain and various parts of organs—to their children and the elderly."

When a relative's brain was eaten, if a kuru infection existed, it was transmitted to new victims. The Fore blamed the presence of kuru on sorcery. When they were convinced that cannibalism was the transmitting agent, however, and gave up the practice, kuru was effectively suppressed. No child born since cannibalism ceased has caught kuru.

Recent Pacific environmental research suggests that the Rapanui were not entirely to blame for what happened, that what might seem the selfish, blind consumption of a precious resource, trees, was not the whole story. A number of variables have been identified as leading to ecological fragility of islands in general. Among them are small size, isolation, latitude, altitude, soils, and rainfall levels. Easter Island possesses all the variables. As Van Tilburg noted: "Rapa Nui's deeply vulnerable ecological deck, metaphorically speaking, was stacked against Polynesian settlers."

When ecological disaster struck Easter Island, in the form of massive deforestation, the islanders had no way out, no way to escape the consequences. The results would be tragic.

DEPLETION AND WAR

The geographer Jared Diamond has said that "[t]he overall picture of Easter is the most extreme example of forest destruction in the Pacific, and among the most extreme in the world: the whole forest gone, and all of its tree species extinct." Diamond famously asks, "What did the Easter Islander who cut down the last tree say while he was doing it?" The author speculates: "Like modern loggers, did he shout 'Jobs, not trees!'? Or: 'Technology will solve our problems, never fear, we'll find a substitute for wood'? Or: 'We don't have proof that there aren't palms somewhere else on Easter, we need more research, your proposed ban on logging is premature and driven by fear-mongering?'"

Shawn McLaughlin, however, cautions us in being too hard on the ancient Rapanui. He says:

> We should realize that most islanders probably did not recognize that depletion was taking place. . . . Forest clearance like this may seem rapid by archaeological standards but the perceived change is low over the course of an individual's life span. Since those who survived infancy probably lived to not much older than 30 years, even the most rapid forest depletion would have occurred at a rate of no more than five percent over a typical islander's lifetime. . . . Easter Island could have contributed to deforestation without the islanders being much aware of it.

That said, deforestation did happen, and people, not natural causes, were the main reason. With forest depletion came the loss of protective tree cover, with the soil surfaces fully exposed to extreme climatic conditions. To replace the protective functions of the former palm forest, a new agricultural system came into being, centered on the horticultural technique of stone mulching on the surface. As Mieth and Bork pointed out, "The stones spread out on the soil surface were probably supposed to protect against transpiration and wind, dampen the temperature curve at the surface and give mechanical support to plant growth." It is possible that as many as a billion stones were taken from small quarries and spread out on numerous Easter Island gardens to accomplish this effect. It has been calculated that as many as 100 people, for 400 years, would have been required to cut, transport, and distribute the stones.

Stone mulching aside, as forest degradation continued, Easter Islanders were forced everywhere to occupy areas of ever-poorer soil. As Steven Roger Fischer concluded, "By the late 1500s, upland farms were simply no longer productive: they were abandoned. Whereupon even greater dependence was made on marine resources, which, in turn, then experienced serious depletion."

Easter Island was in a free fall, its ecological sustainability collapsing. As a consequence, social conflict reached alarming heights.

Legend has it that the climax of intersectional fighting, resulting from the competition for diminishing resources, took place in a famous battle in A.D. 1680 between the so-called "Long Ears" and the "Short Ears." The former were the ruling class (Ko Tu'u Aro), who were said to have inserted disks in their pierced earlobes to create long ears. The latter were the working class, the commoners (Hotu Iti). The Long Ears occupied the western part of Easter Island, the Short Ears the eastern section, known as the Poike Peninsula.

The fighting took place at what has been referred to as the Poike Ditch, a low-lying earthen border between the peninsula and the rest of Easter Island. The conflict resulted in defeat for the Short Ears.

All this about the Long Ears and the Short Ears, and the "ultimate" battle between the two island peoples, is legend, and weak legend at that. Such an encounter may never have taken place. That civil war ensued as a result of resource deprivation, however, is well accepted. And as the

Easter Island was once covered with trees, but a combination of variables resulted in deforestation. Wood became scarce on the island, and without the protection of tree cover, the land could no longer sustain agriculture.

warring intensified and dragged out, it took down with it, literally, the moai and its culture of ancestral worship.

DOWN GO THE MOAI

Archaeologist and petroglyph expert Georgia Lee, who has spent years on Easter Island doing exhaustive research, noted that "[a]ll human societies must have some form of religious system to give meaning to human efforts, reduce anxiety, justify moral obligations, and allow man to commune with the supernatural. Religion supports the social order and unites members of society." That said, Easter Island was now experiencing a major religious meltdown. Chiefs and priests had justified their power by claiming connections with the gods in order to ensure perpetual prosperity and abundant harvests. Moai were constructed as a manifestation of elite authority. But now the promises of chiefs and priests were no longer being fulfilled. Military leaders rose to take their place and, as a consequence, drove the island into civil war.

Armed gangs roamed Easter Island. Fighting, robbery, and pillaging broke out not only between various groups, but within each group. One party would attack another, stealing food, killing or kidnapping people, and setting fire to their property. There would then be reprisals, with victims and relatives retaliating. The result was a perpetual cycle of attack and revenge.

In an attempt to avoid defeat and death, many islanders took to caves as refuge. Numerous grotto entrances are almost impossible to detect. Often an underground chamber would be fortified with a stonewalled entryway. As Flenley and Bahn have noted: "Recent excavations in the cave of Ana Kionga, in the southwest part of Easter Island, found that it had been enlarged, purposely fortified, and camouflaged: a small interior chamber had been walled off with stones, and an entrance tunnel built but concealed beneath debris from the enlargement."

The ultimate insult in the island-wide tit for tat that was now taking place was to damage or destroy another family or clan's ahu and moai. Though occasionally ahu, and even moai, had for centuries been disassembled and reused, what was currently taking place on Easter Island, referred to in legend as "the wars of throwing down of the statues," was meant to destroy, for all time, the ancient culture. Groups that had only recently vied with one another to produce now sought to outdo one another in destruction.

Not surprising, however, the toppling of moai was often no mean feat. They could not just be pushed over. Ropes, levers, and many men were required to take a moai down. Paro, the tallest and heaviest statue ever erected on an ahu, was, understandably, the last to crash. While destruction was certainly an easier task than production, it, nonetheless, required a major effort.

The moai toppling itself, however, was often not enough. According to Flenley and Bahn:

> *In many cases, the statues were deliberately beheaded by placing stones where the fragile neck would fall, for decapitation prevented the statue's re-erection. Most were toppled landward, perhaps*

to cover the eyes; in one case, a statue resting face-upward had its eye area completely pulverized, again a task of considerable effort. These attacks on head and eyes probably reflect the location of the figures' mana—they were not just toppled but had their power totally extinguished.

With all this fighting and killing going on, Easter Island's population decreased significantly to as few as 2,000 by some estimates. Yet, the Rapanui persisted. A new religion, manifested through an amazing and unique ritual, would emerge to give hope and meaning to a devastated, but not defeated, people.

Sacred Birdmen

From the time of settlement, birds were seen not only as a source of food but as sacred animals. It was obvious they could do what humans could not—fly off at any time, go anywhere. Their freedom was the envy of all Rapanui with their ability to flee, if only momentarily, an island prison. If gods were in the sky and men were on land, birds represented a bridge between the two, between heaven and earth.

Hotu Matu'a himself was said to have recognized the power and sacredness of birds. As legend would have it, when the island's first king bequeathed land to his sons, he then left his house and went to Rano Kau. At the crater's narrowest cliff point, he stood on two stones and looked out over the islet of Motu Nui, toward Marae Renga (his homeland). Hotu Matu'a then called to four aku-aku in his old home across the sea and said, "Kuihi, Kuaha, Tongau, Opakako, make the cock crow for me." The cock crowed in Marae Renga, and the king heard it across the sea. It was his death signal, so he said to his sons, "Take me away.". . . Thus Hotu Matu'a came to his end and was buried. . .

Of all the Easter Island birds, the frigate holds the place of honor. It is a large, commanding creature, with black plumage and a mesmerizing, brilliant red gular pouch, which inflates during mating. According to Flenley and Bahn: "Frigate birds were important in Pacific cults as far away as the Solomon Islands, being magnificent flyers and also notorious for being territorially and sexually rapacious: the male's red pouch under the beak is blown up like a balloon during courtship and mating." The authors go on to liken the bird's actions to that of the Rapanui at the time of their cultural implosion.

"One can readily understand their significance for the islanders, for quite apart from the importance of the color red, the birds' behavior must have mirrored that of the islanders themselves, raiding and pillaging as a way of life, demolishing their neighbors' nests, and even stealing twigs (perhaps reflecting the islanders' desperation for timber.)"

With collapse of the ancient order, built on deified ancestors and expressed through the carving and erecting of moai, something new was required to take its place. The ancestors had obviously failed to protect the Rapanui from ecological disaster, famine, and the chaos of constant warfare. It was time to relegate traditional deities to myth and legend and to replace them with a powerful, unifying force. It was time to elevate Makemake, the ancient creator god, to prominence and island-wide veneration.

Makemake would now become the primary source of Easter Island's mana. He would be the focus of a new cult, that of the birdman. As a consequence, the religious heart of the island would move from the ahus to a new ceremonial center, one called Orongo, at Rano Kau.

Foremost a fertility god, one who awards the good and punishes the bad, Makemake would be venerated in the form of the frigate bird. "The association of Makemake with bird symbolism," wrote Alan Drake, in *The Ceremonial Center of Orongo,* "is recorded in legend: the god Makemake was gazing at his reflection in water when a bird appeared above. Makemake was startled to see a being with a beak, wings and feathers and so he joined the images of himself and the bird together."

With Makemake now the deity of choice, an annual ceremony took form in which individuals would compete to retrieve the first egg laid by a bird on the offshore islet of Motu Nui. The ritual of the birdman would take on both religious and secular meaning. The first would be based on the ceremonial relation to elements of fertility. The latter was centered on the reality that the winner of the competition would acquire enormous unifying military and political power.

ORONGO

The ceremonial site of Orongo is located on the south edge of the volcano Rano Kau, the latter, without a doubt, one of the most awe-inspiring geological spectacles in the world. Admittedly, if one visits Rano Kau and

When the inhabitants of Easter Island began to suffer from famine as a result of their overproduction of moai, they began to lose faith in the ancestors that were supposed to protect them. New ceremonial centers, like this one near the village of Hanga Roa, were dedicated to other gods.

its surroundings on a cold, rainy day, the effect can be, well, dampening. "If windy, wet, and cold, it [Rano Kau] was miserable," wrote petroglyph expert Georgia Lee about one of her countless visits. "Then the rain comes in sideways with the wind behind it, and we scurried back to the Land Rover, hugging our precious drawings under our rain ponchos to keep them dry."

But, if you are lucky enough to take in Rano Kau and Orongo on a calm, clear, and warm day, the experience can be truly overwhelming, even life changing.

The rim of Rano Kau rises a thousand feet above sea level. On the east, south, and west, sheer cliffs drop into the sea. On the northern side, a grassy slope descends to Mataveri (the site, today, of the island's inter-national airport). "The interior slopes of the caldera are steep and treach-erous with loose talus and a tangle of vegetation," writes Alan Drake. "A fresh water lake containing *totora* reeds lies 656 feet below the rim and measures 0.68 miles in diameter."

Perhaps no one has been better able to convey the awesomeness and spiritual wonder of Rano Kau than Katherine Routledge, writing almost a hundred years ago. "The whole position is marvelous, surpassing the wild-est scenes depicted in romance," the researcher begins.

> *Immediately at hand are these strange relics of a mysterious past [Orongo]; on one side far beneath is the dark crater lake; on the other, a thousand feet below, swells and breaks the Pacific Ocean, it girdles the islets with a white belt of foam, and extends, in blue unbroken sweep, till it meets the ice-fields of the Antarctic. The all pervading stillness of the island culminates here in a silence which may be felt, broken only by the cry of the sea-birds as they circle round their lonely habitations.*

It has been said that there is perhaps no place on Earth from which one can view more distinctly its curvature than when standing on the southern rim of Rano Kau, looking out to sea. Nothing but that curvature limits one's vision.

The Orongo village itself is located on the narrow southern edge of Rano Kau's rim, a thousand feet above the pounding surf. It consists of stone houses constructed of dry-laid, slatelike masonry, with roofs of soil and grass. "The typical stone house at Orongo is constructed of thin flat basalt slabs (*keho*) stacked up and cantilevered with a ceiling of large transverse slabs," notes Alan Drake. ". . . This volcanic stone separates easily into flat slabs, most of them thicker at the center and tapering to the edges."

Out into the ocean, beginning a mile or so from the island cliffs, are located the three islets of Motu Iti, Motu Kao Kao, and, most importantly, Motu Nui. The last of these islets is the largest at 9.6 acres (3.9 hectares), though like the others, it lacks a permanent source of freshwater. Motu Nui, as will be seen, played a central role in the birdman cult. It was also the location where "pre-birdman cult," adolescent initiation rites took

The village of Orongo, located on the rim of the Rano Kau volcano, was an important center for Easter Island's new cult. This religious movement focused on birds, and many rocks in the Orongo are carved with glyphs depicting birdmen.

place. According to Steven Fischer: "Boys of between 13 and 15 years of age were secluded on Motu Nui for months. Then a ceremony was held at Orongo with a *Tangata tapu manu* or 'Bird Holy Man': the boy had his head shaved, then gave the holy man an egg, whereupon the latter

bestowed on the boy a name for insertion in the ritual. Singing and dancing then took place in front of the stone houses."

AN EGG HUNT LIKE NO OTHER

The "pre-birdman cult" was just that, a prelude to what would, in time,
evolve into full-blown birdman worship. From ancient times there have
been ceremonies to commemorate bird arrivals on Easter Island, not only
the coming of the frigate bird but also that of the sooty tern, a tropical
bird that is blackish above and white below (thus the name). From these
celebrations, and as an outgrowth of adolescent initiation rites, about
A.D. 1550 islanders developed the birdman cult. The cult was centered on
an annual ritual that took place every spring (September in the Southern
Hemisphere). A birdman, who would become Makemake's representative
on Earth, was chosen by open competition, that is, by "sport." Each of the
major island clans selected an individual who would compete to be birdman for a year. The winning clan would have the right to rule over the
entire island for the next year.

The competitor was either striving to become a birdman or, more often,
a man representing a clan leader (thus a surrogate, known in Rapanui as
a *hopu manu*). In the latter case, the clan chief would actually assume the
title. As centuries progressed, the competitor became, in effect, a "stunt-
man," risking his life so that his clan chief could become the *Tangata man*,
birdman.

And, to be sure, the contest could be life threatening.

Members of the dominant clans first gathered at Mataveri, where feasting took place. They then slowly wound their way up to Orongo Village.
Anticipating the arrival of flocks of sooty terns (the frigate bird was now,
essentially, nowhere to be found), contestants prepared to descend the cliffs
of Rano Kau, to the sea. "Competitors first threaded down an ancient narrow trail on Rano Kau's sheer 1,000-foot rock face," wrote Steven Fischer.
"They then paddled on reeds a mile out to Motu Nui." In descending,
would-be birdmen often cut and gouged themselves, resulting in profuse
bleeding, not a good portent when paddling out into shark-filled waters.

At Motu Nui, competitors camped out and waited, often for weeks.
Once the sooty terns arrived, competition centered on finding the first
egg laid. The man to gain the egg (often seized from under the indignant
mother) hurriedly tied it to a headband and dived into the sea once more.

Risking death a second time from sharks or drowning, the swimmer paddled back to the Rano Kau cliff.

Of course, the egg holder had to now ascend a thousand feet up Rano Kau to the safety of Orongo. If successful, and if he was a proxy, the victor then handed the tern egg over to his leader. "Everyone who was gathered about then acknowledged this man to be the new *Tangata manu* for the next twelve moons: the incarnation of the bird deity Makemake," wrote Fischer. "For having lost, the failed competitors had to lacerate themselves ritually with *mata'a*-tipped spears."

In carrying out the actual process of gaining and delivering the first egg laid by a sooty tern, clearly men died. Participants fell from the heights of Rano Kau, were eaten by sharks, or succumbed in conflict with other contestants. No question about it, the birdman "sport," so undertaken, could be deadly.

BIRDMAN OF THE YEAR

For the birdman now chosen, the next year would be, at least on a personal level, a mixed blessing. True, the clan he represented would rule Easter Island, exacting tribute, and then some, from every other clan. But for the birdman, himself, what he would be required to endure, day in and day out for a full year, would not necessarily make him the envy of his fellows. Indeed, the losers in the birdman competition, body flaying aside, may have gotten the better deal.

To begin with, the new birdman was required, even before he left Mataveri, to shave his head, eyebrows, and eyelashes and paint his head white. Just how he went about such barbering, even with a sharp piece of obsidian in hand to accomplish the task, is open to question. Most likely, the procedure was not a smooth, pleasant experience.

The birdman next danced down the mountain of Rano Kau, with egg in hand. He hiked to the foot of Rano Raraku, where he would reside in lazy, "luxurious" seclusion in an elliptical house for 12 months. The birdman lived under strict *tapu* (taboo). He was not allowed to wash or bathe himself for the full year of his ascendancy. He could not cut his nails, which grew conspicuously long—like talons. The birdman was not permitted to eat with the mana-laden hand that had touched the egg he had retrieved. Given these bodily restrictions, it is no wonder it was insisted he remain in seclusion.

The birdman now changed his name to one that had been spiritually revealed to him. The new year was named after him.

The egg the birdman had fetched was assumed to have magical powers, to make island food supplies more plentiful. The egg was blown and then hung up in the birdman's house for 12 moons. It could then be thrown into the sea or hidden in a crevice at Rano Raraku. The egg might eventually be buried with its owner.

According to Alan Drake, "It is said that the birdman designated several persons to be sacrificed for the prosperity of his reign and his choice of victims often caused yet another round of wars."

With a year completed, the birdman was said to have returned to ordinary life, though he retained his status for the rest of his days. The swimmer, who had taken all the risks, who had actually retrieved the sooty

RAPANUI TATTOOING

According to Rebecca Stein, anthropologist and author of the book *The Anthropology of Religion, Magic, and Witchcraft*, the word tattoo comes from the Tahitian word, *ta-tu*, meaning "to mark or strike." For the most part, in Western societies, body tattooing has traditionally been associated with three particular social groups: sailors, gangs, and prisoners.

Not so in Polynesia, where tattooing has been widespread for thousands of years. In Polynesia, tattooing was often connected with chiefly or warrior status. The face, neck, torso, back, legs, arms, and top of the head were tattooed. In a society where clothes were hardly required, tattooing was often the most obvious way to adorn the body. Tattooing began on Rapa Nui probably from the time of settlement.

Tattooing involves piercing or cutting the skin and then introducing a pigment into the opening, or wound. According to the History of Tattooing Web site, www.vanishingtatto.com, "Rapa Nui tattooing implements (*ta kona*) were similar to those found elsewhere in Polynesia (a comb of bird bone lashed at a right angle to a wood handle). The comb was dipped in a prepared pigment of charred tern's brown-speckled egg, also received great stature. With a fresh spring season at hand, a new birdman competition would soon commence, and another birdman would be chosen.

BIRDMAN TYRANNY

The birdman cult on Easter Island found artistic expression through the many petroglyphs carved at Orongo. The rock art featured mythical figures that are half human and half frigate bird. The hands, held either close to the chest or outstretched, hold an egg, the key element in the birdman competition. While the thousands of petroglyphs found on the island take many forms, such as sea creatures (octopus, shark, or turtle) and land animals (lizard or chicken), a major category is that of the *tangata manu*, the birdman, found at Orongo. "Every possible inch on Orongo's rocks

ti leaves (Cordyline terminalis) mixed with black nightshade (Solanum nigrum) juice and struck with a mallet into the skin."

While on Easter Island, Katherine Routledge worked with a Rapa Nui nobleman named Juan Tepano. The islander's tattooing is vividly described on the *History of Tattooing* Web site as follows:

> *Juan Tepano's forehead tattoos consisted of six to ten solid vertical stripes. The parallel lines across the forehead and the fringe of dots were the first motifs tattooed on the face. . . . Beneath Tepano's chin and beard (on the throat) is a stylized bird with head turned down, elongated body and wings reduced to four small tattoo lines. This motif, also seen in other abstract versions on the bark cloth figures, is the frigate bird. . . . Also, on the right side of Tepano's spine is a set of nine parallel lines, running vertically and bending to the right at the bottom, reminiscent of a bird swooping downwards with wings outstretched.*

Clearly, on Rapa Nui, full body tattooing was a common occurrence.

After a grueling, intense competition, the winner of the birdman competition would have to live under a strict set of rules for an entire year. He was forbidden to bathe and had to live in seclusion in a house (*above*) on the foot of Rano Raraku.

contains petroglyphs; birdman motifs swirl over the surfaces and intensive superpositioning of designs indicates long-term use and reuse," wrote Georgia Lee in reference to one of her innumerable explorations of the site. "We found late-period birdmen re-carved over earlier style birdmen, and many Makemake faces that represented that god."

It may be that a new birdman petroglyph was made each year to honor the winning contestant.

Of the 473 birdmen petroglyphs identified so far, the vast majority (86 percent) are located at or near Orongo. "There is no orderly arrangement in the way these petroglyphs are grouped and it would be vain to seek any overall plan," wrote anthropologist Alfred Métraux, in 1957. "They are the product of isolated efforts on the part of generations of devout worshipers, who, by this pious labor, sought either to win the favor of the bird god or to thank him for his aid after victory."

The birdman cult, however, did not solve the islanders' problems; it did not bring abundance and stability to the Rapanui people. "Its enduring legacy was the creation of the most grievous hostilities," wrote Steven Fischer.

> *The result was a permanent tyranny by each respective birdman's paoa, thugs who now "lawfully" ranged the island sowing terror. For the following year's competition, the paoa, enjoying Makemake's patronage, were free to punish all islanders who, in their opinion, failed to acknowledge the sanctity of the new Tangata manu, burning down offenders' huts. . . . Birdman's paoa terrorized and plundered all mata [clans] who were simply not strong enough to resist. The birdman cult might have ended open warfare. But it frequently resembled this, with its own flavor of punctuated butchery and intermittent mayhem.*

To some researchers, the Rapanui were destined for trouble from the moment of settlement. It was said that Hotu Matu'a brought with him the seeds of his people's own destruction. "Forests were cut for wood and the land was cleared for agriculture," notes Alan Drake. "The resulting erosion removed the island's soil cover. Productivity declined as the population rose. There was no longer enough wood to build traditional canoes; islanders could not sail to a more fruitful island. The Rapanui were trapped in a declining environment they themselves created."

For Drake (and a few others as well), Orongo and the birdman cult may have represented the last desperate attempt to circumvent the disasters now overtaking the Rapanui. Tragically, at this low ebb in their lives, the people of Easter Island were soon to experience a new challenge, one they were ill prepared to meet. Amid the dark clouds engulfing the Rapanui, white sails would appear on the horizon. Contact with the Western world would not bring salvation; rather, it would result in the very opposite.

Western Contact
and Rapanui Response

If, on a clear day, one hikes to the top of Maunga Terevaka, the highest point on Easter Island, and there slowly twirls 360 degrees in the breeze, he can see, as the saying goes, forever. At this elevation, one beholds the vast ocean, Earth's curvature clearly visible, with the watery horizon falling to the four points of the compass. Everywhere beyond Easter Island, beyond "Earth Island," is the sea: blue, deep, and, above all, lonely.

It is not known, of course, whether anyone was atop Maunga Terevaka on the afternoon of April 5, 1722. But it is amusing, if nothing else, to speculate that on that bright summer day, one or two Rapanui were up on Maunga Terevaka, maybe just enjoying the day. They would have occasionally, but only occasionally, gazed out to sea. After all, why look; what they would have seen was what they had seen all their lives, what their parents, their grandparents, their great-grandparents, and so on, back to the time of settlement, perhaps 50 or more generations, a thousand years, had seen. The Rapanui would have gazed out at—nothing, nothing but the same blue, never-ending blue, expansive sea.

But on this particular afternoon, as an islander looked around, his or her eyes would have miraculously, mysteriously, unexplainably caught something. No doubt, the observing Rapanui would have frozen in place, speechless, finding the moment truly spellbinding.

Before the particular islander could begin to grasp what was being seen, however, he needed first to process that, for the first time, there was actually something to be seen! Nothing had ever been out there before—ever. Now, there were three distinct, strange objects—big, brown, and white—that seemed to be floating on the water. And, whatever they were, they were moving—and coming—his way. A thousand years of solitude will produce such a moment as this—one that is nearly incomprehensible.

CONTACT

On August 21, 1721, Dutch Commander Jacob Roggeveen set out from the Netherlands at the head of a fleet of three ships, the *Arend* (Captain Jan Coster), the *Thienhoven* (Captain Cornelis Bouman), and the *Afikaansche Galey* (Captain Roelof Rosendaal). Sponsored by the Dutch West India Company, Roggeveen was commissioned to search for a land that, in reality, did not exist: the supposed southern continent of *Terra Australis Incognita*. Many geographers at the time believed that such a landmass had to be in order to provide equilibrium to the globe by counterbalancing the weight of lands in the Northern Hemisphere. In reality, the South Pacific contained no such territory, only small, scattered islands, the tips of submerged, extinct volcanoes.

Roggeveen sailed directly down to the Falkland Islands, off the lower east coast of South America. He then passed through the Straits of Le Maire and continued south beyond 60 degrees south to enter the Pacific Ocean. He made landfall near Valdivia, Chile.

The Dutch commander now set sail west, out into the vast Pacific, in search of Davis Island, a small island said to have been discovered by the English buccaneer Edward Davis in 1687. Roggeveen would never find Davis Island. Undeterred in its explorations, however, the Dutch fleet proceeded northwest into the basically uncharted, unknown, and less than placid eastern South Pacific.

In the late afternoon of April 5, 1722, Captain Rosendaal, commanding the smaller and fastest of the fleet's three ships, the *Afikaansche Galey*, sighted an island "to west by south." "All three ships grouped and waited offshore until the following day," Roggeveen was to write in his journal. "This being thus decided, we gave Captain Bouman (of the *Thienhoven*), who was astern, the relevant information and to the land the name of Paasch Eiland [Easter Island] because it was discovered and found by us on Easter Day."

The next day, April 6, the Dutch fleet cruised along the coast of the newly discovered island, noticing smoke inland, an indication of habitation. On April 7, a storm brought lightning, thunder, and rain. Yet despite

Dutch commander Jacob Roggeveen was the first European to discover Easter Island. The Rapa Nui documented his arrival by carving images of his boat into moai.

the tempest, a single islander, using bunched reeds as a raft, swam out to the *Thienhoven* while the ship was still three nautical miles from the coast. The emissary was immediately brought to Commander Roggeveen on the *Arend*. The first Easter Islander to welcome Europeans, indeed, any outsider at all, was, according to fleet records,

> . . . *a man well into his fifties, of the browns, with a goatee after the Turkish fashion, of very strong physique. He was much astonished at the make of our ship and all that belonged to it, as we could perceive from his expressions. As we could not in the least understand each other, we had to make it out from his expressions and signs. We gave him a small mirror, wherein he looked at himself, at which he was very frightened, as also at the sound of the bell. We gave him a glass of brandywine, which he poured over his face, and when he felt the strength of it began to open his eyes wide.*

The islander, who was said to be particularly interested in the ship and its rigging, was, quite naturally, completely naked. "We tied a piece of sailcloth in front of his private parts," the ship report continued, "which wonderfully pleased him."

When the *Arend's* band struck up a tune, the Easter Islander was said to begin dancing with the sailors. It was observed that he was "very peculiarly painted," meaning tattooed.

Reluctantly, the visiting Rapanui eventually departed, paddling back to land. The next day, however, islanders began arriving in droves to all three Dutch ships. They came in small canoes and on bundles of tied reeds. According to Steven Fischer, "Climbing aboard, the Islanders appeared not in the least frightened of the foreigners, as if they had been receiving overseas guests for years. As gifts, they presented living and roasted chickens as well as bananas, which the Dutch gratefully accepted."

As Captain Bouman noted, however, "They [the Rapanui] were big thieves, taking everything that they could lay their hands on. Above all, they grabbed anything of wood: worn brooms, broken spokes, firewood and such things, and jumped overboard with them and swam to the coast."

The Rapanui displayed a penchant, in particular, for headgear. "They began snatching hats and caps off the sailors' heads and springing overboard with them," continued Bouman. "One Islander climbed straight from his canoe into a porthole of the *Afikaansche Galey* to pilfer a table cloth."

The Dutch, evidently, remained unruffled by all the chaos and thievery taking place onboard. The men, after all, had in return received badly needed gifts of fruit, vegetables, and chickens. Such amiability between two unfamiliar cultures was, however, about to be shattered when the Dutch went ashore on April 10, the only day they would spend on Easter Island.

MUSKET MAGIC

That one day, April 10, would be enough, however, to destroy any possible accommodation between Europeans and the Rapanui.

A crew of 137 men, in five sloops, landed at "High Cliffs," probably Hanga ʻo Honu, at seven o'clock in the morning. It was observed that the "Islanders carried no weapons of any kind, but rather approached in masses to welcome them, 'hopping and jumping for joy'—perhaps a ritual dance to welcome the visitors."

With 20 men remaining on shore to guard the sloops, the main landing party began marching inland. Then, according to accounts reported by Steven Fischer: "Suddenly, back on the beach, a single musket shot split the air. Whereupon a cascade of musketry followed. At once the officers, including Roggeveen, turned back to investigate; some 10 to 12 Islanders [including the first Rapanui to have earlier visited the *Arend*] lay dead, around them a larger number of wounded; not one European seemed to be harmed in any way." The remaining islanders, in utter shock at the "musket magic" they had witnessed, had fled to the hills.

Roggeveen was immediately informed that the islanders had tried to steal a musket. Another was said to have attempted to rip a shirt off a sailor. As a result, a scuffle had broken out and the landing party, fearing for their lives, panicked and started firing at islanders at random.

The Rapanui response to the mayhem that struck them seems, at first, curious, but understandable. Terrified, the islanders brought ever more gifts of chickens and bananas. In response, the Dutch "compensated" the Rapanui with a "half piece of Haarlem cloth."

At this point, the landing party made its way back to the beach, where it boarded the five sloops. According to Captain Bouman, "No further incident occurred, so we left like good friends."

"Nothing was further from the truth, of course," observed Steven Fischer. "Only fear, suspicion, and murder had followed the first European footfall."

Back on his ship, Commander Roggeveen immediately ordered an inquiry into the tragic affair. Cornelis Mens, Captain Bouman's officer, was responsible for the initial musket firing—of that there was no doubt. In his report, Bouman highly disapproved of Mens's conduct, "because we landed first and passed through a great number of inhabitants who made room for us, showing great friendliness. The officers were of the opinion that he had acted out of cowardice."

Though, in hindsight, it seems that the Rapanui, not unlike other Polynesians who were visited by Europeans at the time, were less then over-awed by such "alien" encounters than one might first suppose, they were, nonetheless, shocked by the foreigner's ability to inflict "musket magic." It simply could not be explained. "No ancestral spirit could summon such force," wrote Fischer. "Yet these *Tangata hiva*—'men from beyond'—were neither returned spirits nor 'gods.' They were white men with lethal *mana*. And Easter Islanders were vulnerable in a way they had never been before."

Actually, the magic of the musket, though almost impossible to understand technically, would be nothing compared to the incomprehensible affliction the Dutch left upon departure. By 1723 or 1724, 2,000 or 3,000 Rapanui may well have perished from the pathogens, chief among them smallpox and tuberculosis, that the Dutch unintentionally bequeathed and for which the islanders had no immunity. It would be a ruinous story, repeated over and over again, as Europeans continued, throughout the eighteenth century and beyond, to penetrate the islands of Polynesia.

FURTHER ENCOUNTERS

It would be another half century, 48 years to be exact, before European ships again entered Easter Island waters. In 1770, a two-ship Spanish expedition, led by Felipe González de Haedo, set out from Peru under orders from the viceroy to explore and take possession of any islands not already staked by a European power. Arriving at Easter Island on November 15, 1770, González quickly claimed the island for Spain, named it San Carlos, and erected three crosses on the Poike Peninsula to cement the acquisition.

Though there still could be found a few Rapanui who remembered the encounter and tragedy of 1722, the islanders, nonetheless, greeted

González amicably. "A small party came out to welcome the foreign visitors, and within two days of initial contact men and women in large numbers were swimming out to the Spanish ships, where they began trading for trousers, shirts, ribbons, seamen's jumpers, as well as tiny metal crosses," wrote Steven Fischer. The Spanish were under strict orders not to exploit the Rapanui. Under pain of severe flogging, they were forbidden to accept any article from the islanders without returning a gift of equal or greater value.

The Spanish left Easter Island after a six-day visit. They did little exploring of the interior, perhaps in fear of engaging the Rapanui in conflict.

Next to visit Easter Island was the famed English explorer Captain James Cook, arriving from Tahiti in 1774. The captain commanded a crew that was sick and weary and in desperate need of water and nourishment.

LEPROSY ON EASTER ISLAND

The dictionary defines leprosy as "a chronic infectious disease caused by a mycobacterium affecting especially the skin and peripheral nerves and characterized by the formation of nodules or macules that enlarge and spread accompanied by loss of sensation with eventual paralysis, wasting of muscle, and production of deformities." It is not a pretty sight. In 1936, the Chilean government opened a leper colony on Easter Island. Their actions in doing so, while welcome, were long overdue. Leprosy, which was probably imported from Tahiti after 1886, had infected 5 percent of the population by 1914.

In his book, *The Island of the Colorblind*, medical doctor Oliver Sacks quotes Jacques Arago's frightful picture of the disease on Guam, written in the late seventeenth century:

A few hundred yards from Anigua are several houses, in which are kept lepers of both sexes, whose disease is so virulent that it commonly deprives them of the tongue or some of their limbs, and is said to become a contagious distemper. I have delineated two of these unfortunate creatures, exhibiting to the eye

According to author Rhys Richards, "The islanders were alternately welcoming and threatening, light-hearted and cautious. All were noisy. Some proved fair traders, but others were outrageously dishonest in hiding stones in bags of sweet potatoes. Women offered sex for trifling gifts with the knowledge of their men."

The island Cook found in 1774, just four years after the Spanish visit, was considerably diminished from what it had been. Little freshwater was to be had, being brackish at that. Writing in his journal of March 16, 1774, Joseph Gilbert, master on the *Resolution*, one of the expedition's ships, noted: "The land is exceedingly poor, the hills full of stones, of a hungry dry soil incapable of cultivation. . . . No trees of any size sufficient to make more than the helve of an axe, nor any kind of vegetable useful for refreshment. . . . The inhabitants I believe do not exceed a

the most hideous aspect of human misery. One shudders with horror on approaching these houses of desolation and despair. I am persuaded, that by enlarging these paltry buildings, collecting in them all the persons in the island severely attacked by the leprosy, and prohibiting all communications with them from without, they might expel from the country this frightful disease, which, if it does not quickly cause the death of the patient, at least shortens his days, and perhaps leads him to curse them. What a scene, to behold an infant, a few days old, calmly reposing in the arms of a woman devoured by leprosy, who imprudently lavishes on it her caresses! Yet this occurs in almost every house; government opposes no obstacle to it; and the infant, while sucking in its mother's milk, inhales with it death and disease.

While until fairly recently, Easter Island maintained a leprosy hospital, with a small number of patients, in 2005 there were only three individuals with leprosy left. They were of Polynesian extraction and had probably contracted the disease in Peru.

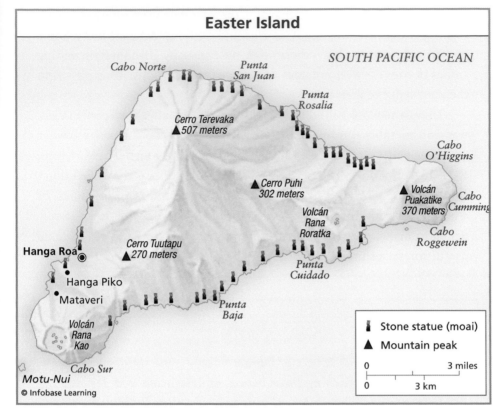

A map of Easter Island.

thousand men. . . . Fish seem scarce, we caught none; no quadruped animals except rats."

Cook, himself, was to have said of Easter Island, "No nation need contend for the honour of the discovery of this island; . . . here is no safe anchorage; no wood for fuel; nor any fresh water worth taking on board." Clearly, in the short years since González's expedition, something terrible had happened on Easter Island. Wars and disease were taking their toll.

In 1786, 14 years after Cook sailed to Easter Island, a Frenchman, Jean-François de Galaup, comte de La Pérouse, arrived with two ships. La Pérouse was, among other things, to gather scientific and ethnographic information and collect animals and plants from the region. Once on shore, La Pérouse and his marines formed a large circle to indicate an inviolable "camp," in which entrance would be strictly limited. Nonetheless, 800 islanders quickly surrounded the camp, at least 150 of which were women and young girls. "Several of these wenches," wrote La Pérouse later, "had a pleasant countenance and offered their favors to each who wished to give them something in exchange. . . . During the time that the females impressed their caresses on us, our hats were stolen from our heads and our handkerchiefs from our pockets."

Although La Pérouse was little impressed with the character of the Rapanui or the island they called home, his geographical engineer, Monsieur Bernizet, was known to have effected a detailed and accurate description of the moai and other island monuments. Thus La Pérouse's gift to island ethnography proved real and welcome and, along with the keen observations of Cook, would inform future explorers and investigators.

RONGORONGO

When the Spanish took possession of Easter Island in 1770, they were able to persuade three leading Rapanui to, as Steven Fischer noted, "take feather in hand, dip it into a black liquid, and then scratch marks on a tapa-like material white as sand and thin as a leaf." In other words, Rapanui, in the view of the Spanish, "signed" away all rights to their homeland.

But how could this be? How could the Rapanui sign anything? Setting aside for a moment that the islanders had no idea what the Spanish "treaty" of succession meant, the real question here is, did the Rapanui have a system of writing? The Rapanui "signatures" consisted of geometric designs and a couple of petroglyph signs. Was this a script? And, if it was, where did it come from? Is it actually possible that the remote, isolated Rapanui had developed a system of writing totally independent of any other?

According to Jared Diamond, writing in *Guns, Germs, and Steel*: "Inventing a writing system from scratch must have been incomparably more difficult than borrowing and adapting one. The first scribes had to settle on basic principles that we now take for granted. . . . They had to devise ways to represent sounds by symbols."

Diamond has concluded that there are only four cases in history where people have invented writing entirely on their own: the Sumerians before 3000 B.C., the Mexican Indians before 600 B.C., the Egyptians about 3000 B.C., and the Chinese by 1300 B.C., with the last two not a firm bet.

The Rapanui, however, may have been a fifth people to do it.

Known as *kohau rongorongo* (literally, "talking wood"), the writing system the Rapanui of Easter Island either invented or drew inspiration

As Europeans continued to explore as much of the world as possible, visitors from other countries came to visit Easter Island. French military leader Jean-François de Galaup, comte de La Pérouse, arrived 14 years after Captain James Cook, and he and his crew studied the island's ethnography.

for from seeing Westerners write, consists of a type of hieroglyphic writing carved on tablets of wood with sharks' teeth or obsidian points. Close to 150 basic symbols have been identified, most of which are anthropomorphic. The key symbols, in turn, are found in some 2,000 compositions. Rongorongo has yet to be deciphered.

The script is not an alphabet. The glyphs are more like "cue cards" for whole words or ideas. It is believed that the glyphs served as mnemonics (memory devices) to facilitate the reciting of oral traditions and genealogies. According to Katherine Routledge, writing in the early twentieth century, an old man told her that "[t]he chanters of the sacred tablets [rongorongo] were members of a special class of priests (*tufunga*) in whose memories were stored island lore."

Reading rongorongo script entails a method know as boustrophedon, from the manner in which an ox plows a field. One starts reading from the bottom left-hand corner, and reading left to right, starts chanting. At the end of a line, the reader turns the tablet around and begins the next line. In another approach, two readers face each other. One reads one line, then the other the next, alternating as they go.

There are said to be only 25 known authentic artifacts incised with rongorongo glyphs in existence. Most of them are on boards 12 to 20 inches long, and together they contain more than 14,000 glyphs. Not one tablet or walking stick with rongorongo is on Easter Island, however—all having been taken to places around the world, such as Washington, D.C., New York, Rome, Paris, Hawaii, and Chile. The origin, purpose, and meaning of rongorongo remains, today, one of the true mysteries of Easter Island.

The Lost Century

Although the three major European expeditions to reach Easter Island in the last third of the eighteenth century (González, Cook, and La Pérouse) made commendable efforts to avoid conflict with the islanders they encountered, that was not the case as a new century dawned and whalers penetrated and permeated the South Pacific. Chief among the interlopers was the American schooner, the *Nancy*, probably captained by the infamous and ruthless J. Crocker of Boston. In 1805, the *Nancy* was engaged in chasing down seals 750 miles west of Chile, on the island of Más Afuera (now Isla San Ambrosio). The captain, not having enough men to capture the marine mammals in quantity, resolved to sail to Easter Island in order to grab whomever he could to "help" with the task.

Landing in what is now called Cook's Bay in early 1806, the captain and crew, after a hard-fought and bloody battle, seized 12 men and 10 women. All were dragged onboard the *Nancy* and put in irons. The schooner quickly left on a return trip to Más Afuera.

According to a report cited by Steven Fischer: "After three days' sailing, the 22 captives were allowed on deck for the first time, and all the men sprang overboard and began swimming back towards Easter Island, well over 200 nautical miles astern. The captain tried to recapture them, but failed. (None would have survived.) The women were taken to Más Afuera, from where they and/or their descendants perhaps emigrated to Chile, Peru, and elsewhere."

There is evidence that the *Nancy* returned more than once to repeat the kidnapping of Easter Islanders.

The *Nancy* would not be the last foreign ship to seek out Easter Islanders and, in the process, inflict atrocities and casualties aplenty. It is said that with dozens of ships arriving at Easter Island between 1722 and 1863, more than 1,000 islanders were hunted down or transported to their deaths by Americans, Europeans, and South Americans. Only one foreigner, in 1856, died at the hands of the Rapanui.

In 1822, another American ship in the business of clubbing seals arrived off Easter Island. According to a trader, J.A. Moerenhout, writing of the incident somewhat later: "When the ship arrived in sight of Easter Island the boats were sent out near the land to procure vegetables, but especially women. They were not long in coming back with as many young girls as there were men on board."

When the crew was done with the Rapanui women, they tossed them overboard to swim back to land. Moerenhout continues:

> *Once back on shore, they were received by groups assembled in a crowd on the shore, and it was then that Waden [the first mate], without provocation and apparently for the sole pleasure of assassination, took his pistol, fired into the midst of them as a form of good bye, with the cunning of the men of his country. One could understand as a consequence the confusion that prevailed about a poor Indian [Rapanui] who fell when a shot had hit him. Waden then ordered the crew to row and go to a distance, with a smile on his face, applauding himself on the justness of his triumph!*

Intimate contact between Easter Islanders and crew members of visiting ships naturally resulted in the spread of venereal disease, particularly syphilis, the scourge of the Pacific. The resulting venereal sterility only served to accelerate an already precipitous decline in the Rapanui population.

A CULTURE IN COLLAPSE

As ever more whalers set foot on Easter Island in the first half of the nineteenth century, "cultural exchanges" increased. Westerners wanted food and freshwater. Islanders were eager to acquire all manner of goods, from clothing to metal to fishhooks to, above all, wood. Visitors were also keenly eager to obtain from the Rapanui their wood carvings, especially statues or "small idols." Since the James Cook expedition, the latter had become a collector's item.

Yet, with food and water a given, it was sex, as noted earlier, that occupants of the visiting ships sought most, with profound consequences all around. "If a crew were denied shore leave, women and young girls were frequently brought on board where they earned trade items for their menfolk," noted Steven Fischer. "In 1830 Captain Waldegrave of H.M.S *Seringapatam* logged that 'the women admitted the embraces of the sailors in the most unreserved manner.' Of the same crew, Midshipman John Orlebar confessed: 'We found that chastity was not in their catalogue of virtues, but certainly, proved with us, I am ashamed to say, their best article of traffic.'"

As a consequence of the ethnic "mixing" now taking place, many offspring of Rapanui and New England American sailors began to appear. So, too, as a result of such "engagements," was the growing prevalence of venereal disease.

In spite of the venereal sterility that many Rapanui women faced, it seems the population of Easter Island had recovered significantly from the eighteenth century pandemics and island-wide warfare. Approximately 5,000 to 6,000 people now occupied Easter Island, with cultivation abundant and trade items from visiting ships diffused throughout the local culture. One account, probably written by Edward Dobson in 1821, and published by Fischer for the first time, noted: "Upon the whole these Islanders appeared a very friendly and inoffensive race of people, the color copper, their hair black and dark brown, but not woolly, they were made and had neither the thick lip or flat nose, but their countenance resembles Europeans, their bodies were tattooed."

The Rapanui had gained a reputation, starting with the first Western visit by Roggeveen in 1722, as having a natural proclivity for a loud, cheerful gregariousness and, for the most part, welcoming nature.

Yet, all was not well on Rapa Nui as the nineteenth century wore on. The islanders suffered from daily want. Life was a constant, immediate struggle. Marauding bands of thugs kept everyone on edge and, in many cases, hiding out, mostly in caves. According to a well-known story, when one clan claimed that another had eaten one of their women, they, in turn, trapped 30 members of the offending clan in a cave and "consumed them in revenge."

In an excellent summary of the tragedy now facing the Rapanui, Van Tilburg declared, "The period of Rapa Nui prehistory from at least A.D. 1680 and extending into the historic era was one in which jealousies and rivalries over land, food, status and women, grudge fights, revenge taking and other negative social interactions appear to have resulted in the need for individuals and families to run and hide, to defend their property and possessions, to threaten to attack their neighbors, and to take individual lives."

Foreigners, to be sure, played a significant role in facilitating what was now, at mid-century, clearly an island culture in collapse. As Fischer points out, "The Island's small population and extreme isolation meant that it could never be anything more than a pawn in a much larger, fiercer game of imperialist exploitation."

That abuse by outsiders was, by the early 1860s, about to achieve ruinous proportions.

THE RAPE OF RAPA NUI

In late 1862, seven (some accounts mention eight) Peruvian ships left the South American continent, sailing west into the open Pacific. They were not whalers; nor were they sealers. And they were not, in the more benign sense, traders. The Peruvians were raiders, plunderers in search of human cargo. They left their homeland, destined for Polynesia, seeking slaves. Their first island stop, given it was closest to the Peruvian coast, would be Easter Island.

According to Steven Fischer, "'Blackbirding,' or kidnapping, was the most heinous series of crimes ever perpetrated against Easter Islanders. Peru was to blame, its name still anathema to East Polynesians because of the outrage."

Peru, like most South American countries, had abolished slavery. The result, however, was a shortage of labor. When the deficiency could not be filled with cheap, imported Chinese labor, slaves, once more, became an economical alternative.

With the Peruvians having arrived off the Easter Island coast, "[a]bout 80 seamen assembled on the beach at Hangaroa while trade goods such as necklaces, mirrors and other items were spread out," explains Georgia Lee. "At a signal, guns were fired and islanders were caught, tied hand

The Rapanui presented themselves as warm and welcoming people, but they were constantly struggling to survive on the island. Without enough resources and food, there were always fights and problems among the island's inhabitants. Above, a nineteenth-century Rapanui man.

to foot, and carried off to the ships. . . . The total Rapanui who were kidnapped was 1,407 or about one-third of the estimated population."

In a further elaboration marking the most fateful day in Easter Island history, adventurer Thor Heyerdahl noted:

> *So it was that on Christmas Eve of 1862 Easter Island lay desolate and depopulated. All who were not lying dead on the rocks by the shore or below decks out in the bay with their hands bound behind them, had crept down into their subterranean catacombs and rolled stones in front of the openings. An oppressive silence reigned on the treeless island. . . . The expressions of the giant gods remained unmoved, but from ships there was cheering and shouting. The visitors did not weigh anchor till they had celebrated Christmas.*

It is also worth noting that the year 1862 marks the last time a birdman ritual was held.

International protests soon ensued, convincing the Peruvian government that if it did not attempt to return what slaves it had taken, the government's reputation would be irretrievably damaged. In response, Peru packed an unseaworthy ship, the *Barbara Gomez* (built to carry 150 passengers), with 470 Polynesians. By the time the ship was ready to sail, on August 18, 1863, 162 islanders had died. On board were 100 Rapanui, of which only 15 survived the journey to Easter Island. At least one returning islander came laden with smallpox.

The resulting epidemic decimated Easter Island's remnant population of approximately 1,500. It was later reported that so many Rapanui had died that it was not possible to bury them all. By 1877, the population would fall to but 110 Rapanui.

Easter Island was clearly dying. According to one summary: "The king, the wise men, the members of the priestly class, those who were the historians of their people had all died, taking with them the enigma of the talking boards [rongorongo], the mysteries of the statues, and the very origins of their ancestors."

MISSIONARY ZEAL

On January 2, 1864, in a determined effort to spread the word of God to the now devastated Rapanui, French Catholic lay brother Eugène Eyraud, representing the religious order Société de Picpus, arrived on Easter Island, having ventured from Tahiti with a few returning Rapanui. Though arriving with all the equipment necessary to set up a simple mission, within no time the novice Eyraud was robbed of all his possessions, including most of his clothes. The missionary, the first foreigner to actually live on Easter Island, would remain for nine months, abandoned by supporters in Tahiti and a virtual captive of the Rapanui.

Brother Eyraud appeared on Easter Island in time to witness the island's greatest cultural upheaval. Tremendous adjustment was required after the massive slave raiding, which saw the capture or death of chiefs, priests, parents, and children. Among this devastation, there was the problem of reassigning lands that no longer had owners. That the island was experiencing massive trauma there is no doubt.

Nonetheless, even with practically nothing to work with and facing constant hostility, Eyraud, with blind dedication, went about his mission to convert the Rapanui. He first set up a school, hoping to instruct

SAVING SOULS

In the nineteenth century, missionaries came to Easter Island and many other parts of Polynesia to "save" the islanders. In many cases, they were there in an attempt to counter the cruelty and subjugation the Polynesians had been experiencing from Western powers. In that sense, their actions can be construed as beneficial, the relieving of suffering and pain.

Yet nineteenth-century missionaries were not anthropologists. They arrived with an openly ethnocentric view, whereby they used their own culture as a basis for interpreting and judging other cultures. In so doing, missionaries came not to understand what they saw but, in many instances, to destroy it and to replace indigenous beliefs and practices with their own.

Georgia Lee, writing in her book *Te Moana Nui: Exploring Lost Isles of the South Pacific*, sums up missionary zeal as follows:

Missionaries came to do good and save souls; they labored mightily and righteously to bring European order into lives that for centuries had been happily disordered. They swathed

children in Christian prayer. Brother Eyraud admits, however, "that these poor people hadn't the faintest idea of what I was trying to teach them. Moreover, their language lacked the words with which to describe it. To teach them the prayers, I had to learn their language, which was more difficult than you can imagine."

Eyraud found that in spite of all the misery around him, for the most part the Rapanui, particularly the children, were simply bored to death. "These good people, in fact, have nothing to do for twelve months of the year," Eyraud wrote in his journal, published in *Early Visitors to Easter Island 1864–1877*. "One day's work assures them of an abundant harvest of sweet potatoes that will last an entire year. During the other 364 days, they take walks, they sleep, and they go visiting. They also have big gatherings and party continually. When a party finishes at one end of the island, another begins at the other. The nature of the festivities depends on the season."

the women from chin to ankle in shapeless dresses to cover their "shameful" bodies, rearranged villages to fit European patterns, burned sacred carvings and dismantled shrines. They taught [about] sin and prohibited the joyous (and sexy) Polynesian dancing. The South Seas are associated with love, as Bengt Danielsson observes, but the missionaries found the Polynesian attitudes toward sex to be "utterly horrible" and complained that the predominant theme of conversation from youth to old age "is the filthy coition of sexes." Deliberate efforts were made by interlopers to destroy the islanders culturally and change them socially. When the missionaries in the Marquesas insisted that boys caught sleeping with girls had to marry them, it not only upset ancient customs, but it sorely confused the Marquesans.

To be sure, missionary attitudes in the twentieth century became, in many instances, more enlightened. Though Father Sebastian Englert tended to see the Rapanui as children in need of paternal care, there was more than a bit of the ethnographer in him.

Following the explorers, European missionaries soon came to Easter Island to convert the Rapanui to Christianity. The islanders, whose population was depleted from disease and recent tragedies, received their first residential missionary in 1864 and began to move further away from their beliefs in the moai.

Evidently, cultural trauma notwithstanding, at least some Rapanui found time enough to kick back and play.

In September of 1864, Eyraud was "rescued" and brought to Chile. He returned, however, in March of 1866 under the leadership of an older, even more determined missionary, Father Hippolyte Roussel, a man not to be trifled with. Roussel carried a big cane with a lead head. When threatened by a Rapanui, Roussel would respond, uninhibitedly, with his "weapon."

Later in 1866, two more missionaries joined Eyraud and Roussel. "For the disheartened islanders, the food and medicines provided by the missionaries were an incentive for conversion," wrote Georgia Lee. "Such exotics as wheelbarrows, horses, other animals were introduced. They converted the islanders and introduced them to a Western lifestyle." Nonetheless, the Rapanui continued to suffer from introduced diseases. Eyraud, in August of 1868, died of tuberculosis and was buried on the island. Before his demise, he undoubtedly infected many Rapanui with the disease.

In the 18 months between Eyraud's departure in 1864 and his return with Roussel in 1866, Easter Island experienced, party time aside, yet another long round of fighting, house burnings, destruction of crops, and widespread famine. The missionaries may have saved some souls, but they could not stop the continued decimation of a people and their culture.

THE TYRANT

It would not be long before an enterprising foreigner was quick to visualize opportunities on Easter Island, a land far from trade routes, little populated, and, most telling, lacking any European jurisdiction. That man would be a French sea captain and former Crimean Army officer, Jean-Baptiste Onèsime Dutrou-Bornier. It would be hard to find a more opportunistic, cunning, self-serving European to ever set foot on Easter Island, with the purpose of making the entire island his home. In 1865, after abandoning his wife and child in Paris, Dutrou-Bornier headed for Tahiti. Three years later he sailed, with a handyman named Christian Schmidt, for Easter Island.

Dutrou-Bornier set to work buying up more and more land in exchange for minor goods, such as tools and cloth. Eventually, he hoped to ship islanders (for a price) off to Tahitian plantations. Every month Dutrou-Bornier enlarged his estate, and he soon built a fancy wooden house, the volcanic foundations of which came from ancient sites.

Where and how Dutrou-Bornier found the wood (on a treeless island) to build his house is a tale that reveals all one needs to know about this most devious of men. According to Georgia Lee, "When ships arrived at the island, Dutrou-Bornier would row out and advise them where to anchor to prevent being blown onto the rocks if the winds changed. He deliberately misled visitors so that when the winds did change, ships went aground." Dutrou-Bornier would then salvage the lumber for use in constructing his house.

It was not long before Dutrou-Bornier and his armed allies found themselves in conflict with the missionary settlement on Easter Island. The latter objected to Dutrou-Bornier's land grabbing and claim of authority over the Rapanui. Dutrou-Bornier, however, had the weapons, including a salvaged cannon. The missionaries, no match for the island's new tyrant, departed in the years 1870 and 1871.

For many Rapanui, the only way out of all the chaos around them was escape. On June 6, 1871, in what Steven Fischer calls "one of the saddest days in Rapa Nui history," more Rapanui left the island than remained. When Captain Schaffer, of the *Sir John Burgoyne*, arrived to take the fleeing Rapanui away (the majority bound for Tahiti), "The entire population crowded the shore in order to leave the island on his vessel. But he could take only 275 aboard, meaning that some 230 had to be left behind . . . who were now weeping and wailing for their departing loved ones, most of whom they would never see again."

As was noted earlier, by 1877 the population of Easter Island had fallen to 110 Rapanui. Ironically, in the same year, a few islanders took matters into their own hands, ambushing and murdering Dutrou-Bornier and thus ending his tyrannical rule.

In 1888, the Chilean government, seeking a place on the world stage defined, in part, by the acquisition of colonies, took formal possession of Easter Island. They did so more or less by default—no other country, it seems, wanted the place. Upon hearing the rumor of Chilean annexation, more than a hundred Rapanui, living in exile and in poverty on Tahiti, made plans to return to their homeland. Perhaps they felt within them the spirit of Hotu Matu'a. The king, undoubtedly, would have been heartened.

Research
and Renewal

With the annexation of Easter Island in 1888, Chile became a colonizing power. Just what it should do with its new acquisition, however, would be an ongoing problem for the South American country. Plans for a naval base and harbor went nowhere. Initially, the Chilean government simply decided to lease the island out to allow it to become, in effect, one vast, commercial sheep ranch. The founding rancher in this endeavor, a man named Enrique Merlet, would soon, through his tyrannical rule, become every bit as hated as Dutrou Bornier ever was.

Merlet's first task was to form the company La Compañía Explotadora de la Isla de Pascua (the company to exploit the island). The company brought up to 500 "starter" sheep and took over the Dutrou-Bornier site at Mataveri, making the place its headquarters. In March of 1896, Alberto Sánchez Manterola, the first on-site manager, arrived to take control of island property. "Beginning with Sánchez in 1896, company managers on Easter Island were like captains of a ship: some despotic, all of them firm, none paternal," wrote Steven Fischer. "Allegiance lay solely with the company. Rapanui and their culture meant little or nothing at all. A profitable wool-clip was everything, and how to achieve and maintain steady growth."

Over the next two years, exploitation of the Rapanui by island managers and their hired hands grew to frightening proportions. Virtually all grassland locations on the island were cleared for livestock, and the Rapanui themselves were ordered to live at or near Hanga Roa. "The Rapanui world shrank, as the 'company world' grew," Fischer noted.

Then, in the greatest humiliation to visit the Rapanui short of slavery, Sánchez had his laborers (the Rapanui, of course) build a 10-foot-high wall, topped with wire, around Hanga Roa, eventually to enclose 2,471 acres (1,000 hectares). All Rapanui were ordered to remain within the wall unless they were out on company business elsewhere on the island. Like island livestock, the Rapanui were confined within an enclosure.

Initially, the Rapanui did not realize they were building what would be, in effect, their concentration camp. They were grateful, at first, as Fischer pointed out, "[to] earn hard cash. For this enabled them to purchase, in the company's primitive store, the imported cloth, tobacco and sugar they didn't need, at prices they couldn't afford. . . . And no one would have believed that only their grandchildren would experience the Wall's toppling—more than half a century later."

By the turn into the twentieth century, the Rapanui had become prisoners on their own island. All were forbidden to leave their homeland. Incoming visitors were told not to discuss the outside world with islanders.

In 1908, a new manager arrived, an Englishman named Henry Percy Edmunds, equally as severe as any before him, but, by most accounts, more just and humane. Edmunds would eventually learn the local language and, in going about his management duties, was more than willing to get his hands dirty. Having been a dealer of artifacts in Europe, Edmunds was quick to recognize the commercial possibilities of Easter Island's wood carvings. He set the Rapanui scurrying about, from cave to cave, in search of originals, while he had others carve reproductions.

In April of 1911, perhaps to some extent as a result of Edmund's interest and his publicizing of Rapanui cultural treasures, a Chilean scientific expedition arrived on Easter Island, the first of its kind to take a serious, scholarly interest in the remote location. The expedition stayed for 12 days, establishing a meteorological station and a seismic register. Its efforts would be but the beginning in a long century of island inquiry to come.

KATHERINE ROUTLEDGE

On March 25, 1913, Katherine Routledge, along with her husband, William, and a crew of 10, set sail in a custom-built, 90-foot-long schooner, the *Mana*, from Falmouth, England, on the trip of a lifetime. Routledge, one of the first women to graduate from Oxford University, would also be the first woman archaeologist to work in Polynesia.

Born into a wealthy English Quaker family, Routledge and her equally well-off husband had the financial means to have their own boat built to specifications and then to sail it anywhere in the world. Having spent a number of years in British East Africa, the Routledges were now on a quest to explore and study one of the most remote places on earth—Easter Island. Sailing around Cape Horn, it would take the *Mana* a year to reach its destination. On March 29, 1914, the Routledges and their crew arrived at Easter Island, where they immediately set up two base camps, one in the area of Mataveri and the other at the statue quarry of Rano Raraku. Katherine Routledge would remain on the island for 17 straight months.

The *Mana* sailed with the support of the Royal Geographical Society (among other British scientific organizations), which placed a high premium on the adventurer-anthropologist Routledge team finding and deciphering rongorongo inscriptions. The two were also charged with gaining an understanding of the island's ancient human origins. Katherine Routledge would be particularly interested in the moai and would carry out the first-ever extensive cataloging of their type and numbers. "Katherine learned the language and interviewed elderly islanders, studied the ruins, excavated statues, and rode horses across the rugged landscape," Georgia Lee wrote admiringly of Routledge. "Her notes (and subsequent book) have proved to be a gold mine for scholars over the years. In part due to Routledge's work, the incredible rock art and archaeological wealth of this remote island began to fascinate and attract travelers and research expeditions."

During Katherine Routledge's 17-month stay on Easter Island, she not only observed and studied its history; she became, in one clear incident, part of it.

The Rapanui were not faring well on their island, a result of the abuse and confinement they were made to endure. As a consequence, a woman named Angata, a prophetess, announced that she had had a dream that Easter Island once again belonged exclusively to the Rapanui. Soon enough, Angata led a band of rebelling Rapanui out, through the town wall, on a rustling mission. "That night the bonfire of joyous feasting, on the flesh of slaughtered cattle, illuminated the Hanga Roa church," wrote Steven Fischer. Before long, it was clear the Rapanui were bent on taking their island back.

As violence increased and the situation deteriorated, Katherine Routledge, who had earlier befriended Angata, tried to mediate the situation. The deliberations did not succeed, and soon Katherine Routledge and other foreigners on the island began to fear for their lives.

On August 5, 1914, a ship, the *Banquedano*, arrived to restore order. Though the rebellion had obviously failed, the ship's captain, Almanzor Hernández, ruled that the Rapanui had been fully justified in doing everything they had done.

On August 18, 1915, Katherine Routledge left Easter Island. Back in England, she would give slide shows and lectures about her experiences. In 1919, her book, *The Mystery of Easter Island*, was published. It remains one the most authoritative and insightful accounts ever written about Easter Island.

MR. KON-TIKI

Katherine Routledge, though not a trained archaeologist, had, by her extensive and credible work, set the stage for fully credentialed investigators to come.

In 1934, the Franco-Belgian expedition of ethnologist Alfred Métraux and rock art enthusiast Henri Lavachery arrived on Easter Island. The team would do extended follow-up work to what Katherine Routledge had initiated. At the time, the Rapanui population stood at 454.

In 1935, two significant events took place. The Chilean government declared the Isla de Pascua (Easter Island) a national park and historic monument. As a consequence, no artifact could henceforth be removed from the island, and every expedition hereafter would require a government license.

Also, 1935 saw the arrival of the German priest Sebastian Englert. He would remain for decades on the island, not only learning the Rapanui language, but studying it extensively. In addition to the pastoral care he provided, Englert represented a permanent scholarly presence on Easter Island. The paternalistic priest would have considerable influence on the islanders he quickly came to love.

In 1936, a naval office, radio station, leper colony, and drugstore were built on the island. The Rapanui population was growing, albeit slowly, reaching close to 500.

In the early twentieth century, researchers studying the Rapanui and the moai garnered a great deal of attention. Hoping to protect sites like this longboat-shaped house foundation, the Chilean government classified the island as a national park and historic monument.

In 1937, the Chilean government tried to sell Easter Island to a foreign power. While there was some interest in acquiring the island, negotiations fell through.

In 1952, with a population of between 700 and 845, it is still worth noting that but one supply ship visited Easter Island annually. Its appearance, as can be expected, was eagerly awaited by all islanders.

Given the paucity of visitors to Easter Island, it is no surprise that when, in 1955, the Norwegian expedition led by famed archaeologist/adventurer Thor Heyerdahl, "Mr. Kon-Tiki," showed up for an extensive stay, islanders were ecstatic. Arriving on the Norwegian ship *Christian Bjelland*, on October 27, 1955, and remaining on the island until April 6, 1956, the expedition would, among other things, have a profound effect in introducing Easter Island to the outside world.

Thor Heyerdahl came to Easter Island with an agenda. In 1947, he and a small crew built a raft (Kon-Tiki) and sailed it from the coast of South America to the Thamotu Islands (a 3,000-mile journey). His purpose in doing so was to convince skeptics that the eastern Polynesian islands were settled, not from the west, but from the east, from South America. Heyerdahl failed to convince scholars of his theory, and, today, DNA evidence has completely debunked the notion. Still, Heyerdahl and his crew on Easter Island, a number of whom were independent archaeologists who did not necessarily subscribe to the explorer's position on Easter Islander origins, did valuable investigative work during their five-month stay. In addition, Thor Heyerdahl seems to have had the time of his life exploring and investigating the mysteries of Rapa Nui.

Caves were of particular interest to Heyerdahl, something Easter Island had in abundance. "When the rest of our party were well under way with the excavations, we saddled four horses and the photographer and I, with Eroria and Mariana, rode off to reconnoiter caves," wrote Heyerdahl in his enormously popular book illuminating his Easter Island adventures, *Aku-Aku*.

> *On the first day we were in and out of dark caves from morning till night. Some were quite open, and we could bend down and walk in. Others were carefully blocked up with stones, so that only a little rectangular opening was left through which we could crawl in on all fours. But most of them were mere rat-holes, into which we could neither walk or crawl, but had to push our legs in with stiff knees and keep our arms stretched over the head while wriggling the body like a snake through a long and horribly narrow shaft. . . . In most of these caves the roof was so low that we had to stoop, and in some we could only stand doubled up or merely sit.*

There is a reason why Thor Heyerdahl is known as having been both an archaeologist and an adventurer.

THE MONEY ECONOMY

While on Easter Island, Heyerdahl and his crew were able to reerect a single moai, *Ature Hiki*, at Anakena. Five years later, however, American archaeologist William Mulloy, who had been part of the Heyerdahl expedition, began what would be an extensive, decades-long statue reerection project. The final aspect of this endeavor would take place long after Mulloy's death in 1978. From 1992 to 2002, the reconstruction, reerection, and full restoration of Easter Island's largest ritual complex, the majestic *Ahu Tongariki* site, with its 15 moai, was completed, with the aid of a modern, imported Japanese crane.

Life on Easter Island was changing. In 1966, the Rapanui became Chilean citizens, and the population reached 1,100. And, in a truly significant event that opened the island to the outside world and the tourism that would launch the islanders headlong into the money economy, an airport was constructed in Mataveri. An inaugural commercial flight took place on April 2, 1967.

Using prop-driven airplanes, the subsequent monthly LAN Chile flights from Santiago took nine hours to get to Easter Island, slow by today's standards, but a lot faster than by boat. In 1970, LAN Chile began using Boeing 707 jets, cutting flight times nearly in half. By the following year, flights of tourists were coming in twice a week. Today, commercial airplanes arrive almost every day on Boeing 767 jets.

The ability to land ever larger planes (jumbo jets) on Easter Island took a giant leap forward when, in 1986, Mataveri International Airport, thanks to American money, had its runway extended to 10,000 feet, giving it one of the longest airstrips in the world. The extension, curiously, was not carried out for commercial reasons, though the commercial effect of the ability to land aircraft of any size would be significant. The island runway was lengthened to provide an emergency landing site for the American space shuttle. At the time, there were plans to launch the space shuttle from Vandenberg Air Force Base in California into polar orbit, in which case an emergency touchdown might have been required somewhere in the South Pacific. The shuttle was never launched from the West Coast of the United States, thus the rocket plane never landed on Easter Island. Had it done so, however, no doubt "ancient astronaut" enthusiast Erich Von Däniken would have been pleased.

In 1993, when the Rapanui population had reached 3,000 plus, Hollywood arrived on Easter Island. The filming of the movie, *Rapanui*, produced by Kevin Costner, would have an enormous impact on the island's rapidly developing money economy.

"Instead of a few weeks on the island [as was the case with earlier documentary filmmakers], the film crews stayed on the island for six months and nearly every islander worked on the movie, in some category," wrote Georgia Lee. "The Rapanui made very good money. That was the good news. The bad news: they all bought cars, motorcycles, and trucks with their earnings. Now the island has some 4,000 vehicles and traffic jams on the main street, and the village has a whole age-group of small boys with the name 'Kevin.'"

For centuries, Easter Island has been referred to as the most remotely inhabited place on Earth. But one has to ask what that really means today, when a visitor can fly from urban, sophisticated, cosmopolitan Santiago to Easter Island in five hours, the same time it takes to fly from urban, sophisticated, cosmopolitan San Francisco to Hawaii. Within 15 minutes of landing at Mataveri International Airport, one can be chatting

EASTER ISLAND MYTHS DEBUNKED

A myth can be seen as a traditional story of an ostensibly historical event, a popular belief or tradition that has grown up around something or someone. The myth (some would prefer the term *legend*) of Hotu Matu'a as the king who founded Easter Island is a good example. The myth of Hotu Matu'a may or may not be true. We will never know. However, there are myths concerning Easter Island that, though popular and regarded as true by some, are clearly false. Here, from Shawn McLaughlin, in his book, *The Complete Guide to Easter Island*, are but a few Easter Island myths debunked:

+ Easter Island was settled by people from eastern Polynesia, *not* South America. The genetic, osteological, ethnographic, and linguistic evidence is solid on this.
+ The rock from which the moai were carved is *not* so hard it requires lasers to cut it.
+ Moai carving at the Rano Raraku statue quarry did *not* stop abruptly despite the fact that many moai are unfinished and stone tools were found littering the ground. The end of the statue-building cult was a drawn-out process.

in a local Internet café. High school girls walk around Hanga Roa, their faces pointed downward, as they text-message friends on their cellphones. World Cup competitions are shown on flat-screen televisions, via satellite, instantaneously. And island residents, setting aside (at least momentarily) any rumblings about Chilean dominance, go wild when Chile is in the competition.

Yet, no question about it, get up early on a foggy morning, head out of Hanga Roa on the road leading north, drive along the southern coast, out to the Poike Peninsula, and you know you are not in Manhattan, Santiago, or even Hawaii. You are in a different world, a world at once slower, quieter, and more removed from almost any other permanently inhabited place on Earth. And, if you are like most visitors from the "modern"

+ There is no convincing evidence that islanders captured during the nineteenth century Peruvian slave raids were taken to the guano mines of the Chincha islands; they became indentured servants of wealthy Peruvian landowners. But follow-up research is under way.

+ Easter Island is not the last vestige of a lost continent; that theory emerged long before the birth of the scientific method, the now-proved theory of "continental drift," and the mapping of the ocean floor.

+ Yes, the terms *Hanau Eepe* and *Hanau Momoko* were once respectively defined as *Long Ears* and *Short Ears*—but this is *not* what these terms mean. Instead, these terms mean "corpulent" and "thin" and may have associations with social-class distinctions.

+ A common misconception is that *no* trees grew on the island early on; this is not true; before deforestation took effect, there may have been millions of trees on the island.

world, you are glad for the respite, the slower pace, the incredible, inviting silence, and the intoxicating loneliness.

HŌKŪLE'A

Ben Rudolph Finney is one interesting and varied ethnographer. In addition to receiving a Ph.D. from Harvard, the professor of anthropology, at the University of Hawaii, is considered one of the world's leading authorities on—surfing! That said, it is Finney's knowledge of and firsthand expertise in canoe sailing that have made him a leading figure in the study of Polynesia. In 1973, Finney cofounded the Polynesian Voyaging Society. Through the society's efforts, the *Hōkūle'a* was built; the double-hulled canoe would attempt to replicate the long-distance voyaging of the ancient Polynesians, using traditional navigational techniques. The *Hōkūle'a* would, in effect, seek to do what Hotu Matu'a had done a thousand or more years before.

Hōkūle'a is Hawaiian for the bright star Arcturus that shines directly over the island of Hawaii. The canoe, made as far as possible with traditional materials, but, nonetheless, required to use modern components in many cases, was launched in 1975. Anthropologists, maritime historians, and archaeologists collaborated on the vessel's design, enabling it to simulate an ancient Polynesian craft in shape, weight, and performance. Because there was no Polynesian alive who knew how to navigate the craft in the traditional way, Mau Piailug, a navigator from the Caroline Islands of Micronesia, was selected to steer the canoe, using the stars, ocean swells, and the various indicators ancient oceanic peoples were familiar with.

Hōkūle'a's inaugural voyage, in 1976, took it from Hawaii to Tahiti and back. According to the Wayfinders: A Pacific Odyssey Web site:

> *Navigator Mau Piailug used the rising points of the stars, supplemented by observations of the sun, moon, and ocean swells, as a natural compass to guide the canoe [Hōkūle'a]. Even when days of solid cloud cover hid the stars, sun and moon from sight, Mau was able to keep the canoe on course and keep in his mind an accurate picture of the canoe's progress toward Tahiti. And, obligingly, small, white fairy terns skimming over the sea, told Mau that the atoll of Mataiva, just to the north-northwest of Tahiti, was near before it could actually be*

Although the moai have remained the same since their creation, the rest
of Easter Island has changed around them. The Rapanui have adapted to
modern times, but they continue to preserve their unique culture and heritage.

*seen. Once this atoll had been reached, it was easy to orient the canoe
for the short sail to Tahiti.*

The voyage of the *Hōkūle'a* from Hawaii to Tahiti and back effectively
demonstrated that ancient Polynesian canoes, using traditional navigation methods, were up to the task of long-range Pacific travel.

The *Hōkūle'a* would eventually complete nine voyages to places such
as Micronesia, Japan, Canada, and the United States, all the while using
ancient wayfinding techniques and celestial navigation. In addition, the
Hōkūle'a would spawn a renaissance in the construction of Hawaiian sailing canoes, as well as those of the Tahitians and New Zealand Maori.

In 2000, the *Hōkūle'a* sought, successfully, to "close the triangle," that
is, the Polynesian Triangle, by sailing from Hawaii to Rapa Nui, via the
Marquesas Islands. On the way, a brief stop was made at Pitcairn Island. It
was then on, over a thousand miles upwind, to Rapa Nui. Surely, the spirit
of Hotu Matu'a must have accompanied the adventurous crew.

In a time when many contemporary Polynesians are culturally adrift, neither completely in the modern world that is overwhelming them nor anchored in the memory of their incredible seafaring past, the voyaging of the *Hōkūle'a*, and particularly its journey to far-off Rapa Nui, has given them a renewed sense of pride. "In this situation, the reconstruction and sailing of ancient voyaging canoes becomes more than adventurous and anthropologically-fruitful excursions into the past," the Wayfinders: A Pacific Odyssey Web site declared. "These projects become ways culturally-uprooted Polynesians can themselves rediscover the means by which their islands were discovered and settled, indeed their ancient cultural heritage as a uniquely oceanic people."

Though, today, there are no pure Rapanui left on Easter Island (or anywhere else in the world), that does not mean the islanders are lacking in Polynesian pride—far from it. In a confused and challenging modern world, Easter Islanders can move forward knowing they are part of an incredible past. Keeping, holding on to, and celebrating their heritage will be, amid all commercial pressures around them, a real challenge. It is hoped that the Rapanui will find a way to preserve, enhance, and magnify their amazing cultural inheritance, neither for the tourist dollars it will bring in, nor even for the scholars who come to study the island, but for themselves, for their own unique place in the "navel of the world."

While many of the mysteries of Easter Island have now been solved, the island still provides abundant mystery in the full sense of the word. One may have to go out of his or her way to reach Rapa Nui, but it is well worth the effort. And when a visitor finally does arrive, Hotu Matu'a's decendants will be waiting with a warm Polynesian greeting.

Chronology

c.3,000,000 ago	Poike, the first volcano to create Easter Island erupts.
c.2,000,000 ago	Rano Kau, the second volcano to create Easter Island erupts.
c.300,000 ago	Terevaka, the third volcano to create Easter Island erupts.
c. 30,000 ago	Buka, in the Solomon Islands of Near Oceania, settled.
c.13,000 ago	Manus Islands settled.
c.400–1000	Islanders first arrive, the first ahu is constructed, and deforestation begins.
c.1000–1680	Moai erected on ahu.
c.1680–1722	No moai built, many toppled; opposition between east and west territories increases.
1722	*April 5:* Dutch Commander Jacob Roggeveen discovers Easter Island.
1770	*November:* Don Felipe González visits Easter Island, claims it for Spain.
1774	*March:* Captain James Cook visits Easter Island, reports toppling of moai.
1805	Crew of American schooner *Nancy* captures 22 Rapanui, with the 12 men onboard soon jumping overboard to their deaths.
1862	*December:* Peruvian slave-raiding expedition captures 1,400 Rapanui, one-third of the island's population. The last birdman ritual is held. The population is reduced to 3,000.
1863	Smallpox epidemic decimates the population.
1864	Arrival of first missionary from Valparaiso.
1866	Dutrou-Bornier arrives.

1868	H.M.S. Topaze removes two statues, later presented to Queen Victoria.
1877	The population is down to 110 Rapanui.
1888	Chile annexes Easter Island.
1897	Mr. Merlot of Valparaiso leases the greater part of the Island.
1914	Katherine Routledge arrives on the *Mana*. Island revolt.
1934	Archaeologist Alfred Métraux arrives.
1935	Rapa Nui National Park established.
1955–1956	Thor Heyerdahl's Norwegian expedition on the island.

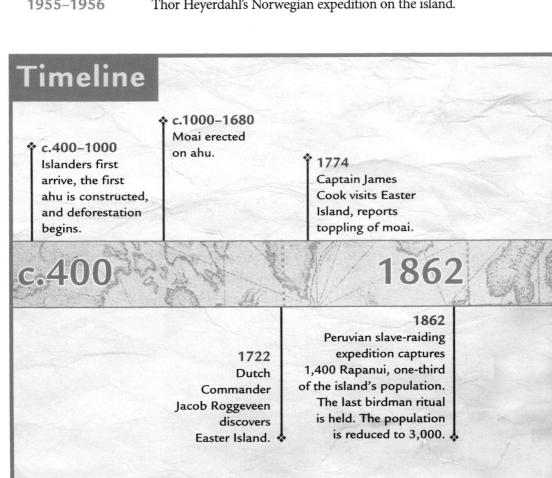

Timeline

❖ **c.400–1000**
Islanders first arrive, the first ahu is constructed, and deforestation begins.

❖ **c.1000–1680**
Moai erected on ahu.

❖ **1774**
Captain James Cook visits Easter Island, reports toppling of moai.

c.400

1862

1722
Dutch Commander Jacob Roggeveen discovers Easter Island. ❖

1862
Peruvian slave-raiding expedition captures 1,400 Rapanui, one-third of the island's population. The last birdman ritual is held. The population is reduced to 3,000. ❖

1966	Chile declares Easter Island a province.
1967	Mataveri airport opens.
1969	Tahai restored by Mulloy.
1986	NASA program extends the island's airstrip.
1993	A major Hollywood film, *Rapa Nui*, is produced on the island.
1996	UNESCO declares Easter Island a World Heritage Site.
2000	The *Hōkūleʻa* arrives on Easter Island, having sailed from Mangareva.

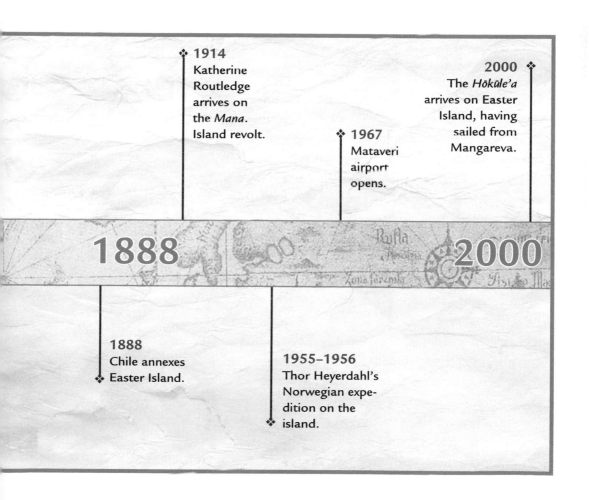

❖ 1914
Katherine
Routledge
arrives on
the *Mana*.
Island revolt.

❖ 1967
Mataveri
airport
opens.

2000 ❖
The *Hōkūleʻa*
arrives on Easter
Island, having
sailed from
Mangareva.

1888

2000

1888
Chile annexes
❖ Easter Island.

1955–1956
Thor Heyerdahl's
Norwegian expe-
dition on the
❖ island.

Glossary

ahu   Sacred site for honoring ancestors, the most important area of which is a large platform constructed from huge stone blocks, filled with a mixture of earth and rock.

ancestor worship   The veneration of ancestors, who may bring aid to their descendants or, if neglected, may bring misfortune.

anthropology   The study of humanity.

anthropomorphic   Having a human form or human attributes.

archaeologist   A person who digs up, studies, identifies, and sometimes removes evidence of prehistoric cultures.

archipelago   An expanse of water with many scattered islands.

Ariki   Men who were believed to possess supernatural powers that they used to benefit the community.

boustrophedon   The writing of alternate lines in opposite directions.

caldera   A volcanic crater that is formed by the collapse of the central part of the volcano or by explosions of extraordinary violence.

creator god   A god that is responsible for the creation of the physical earth and the plant and animals that live upon it.

ethnocentrism   Using one's own culture as the basis for interpreting and judging other cultures.

ethnography   The descriptive study of human societies.

guano   Seabird manure, often sought for its use as a powerful fertilizer.

horticulture   The use of cultivated domesticated plants without the use of fertilizers, plows, irrigation, and other agricultural technologies.

legend   A traditional story about past events that is considered to be true; usually contains an element of reality.

mana   An impersonal supernatural force.

mnemonic   Assisting or intending to assist memory.

moai   The large stone statues representing ancestors of a dynasty, made primarily from volcanic rock at the Rano Raraku quarry.

myth   A sacred story that provides the basis for religious beliefs and practices.

pukao   A stone cylinder mounted on the head of some moai to represent a topknot of hair.

rano   A crater lake.

relic   An object of religious veneration.

rongorongo   An undeciphered picture writing on wooden tablets, unique to Easter Island.

schooner   Typically a two-masted fore- and aft-rigged vessel with a foremast and a mainmast stepped nearly amidships.

spirit   A supernatural being that is less powerful than a god and is usually more localized.

surrogate   A person put in the place of another.

syphilis   A chronic, contagious venereal disease.

tabu   Objects and people that are supernaturally prohibited.

talon   The claws of an animal, such as those of a bird.

toromiro   A small tree, the wood from which was often used for carving.

totora   A reed that can be used for thatch.

tuff   Hardened volcanic ash.

wayfinding   The use of traditional, non-instrument celestial navigation techniques to find one's way at sea.

Bibliography

Albee, Edward. "Easter Island: The Dream at the End of the World." *New York Times,* April 30, 2006.

Altman, Ann M. *Early Visitors to Easter Island 1864–1877.* Los Osos, Calif.: Easter Island Foundation, 2004.

Ancient Navigation. Available online. URL: http://www.pbs.org/wgbh/nova/easter/civilization/navigation.html

Bahn, Paul, and John Flenley. *Easter Island Earth Island: A Message from Our Past for the Future of Our Planet.* London: Thames and Hudson Ltd., 1992.

Ball, Ian. *Pitcairn: Children of Mutiny.* Boston: Little, Brown and Company, 1973.

Banks, Joseph. *The* Endeavor *Journal of Joseph Banks 1768–1771.* John C. Beaglehole, ed. 2 vols., vol. 1:368. Sydney: Angus and Robertson, 1962.

Barbour, Jeff. *Blue Planet & Beyond: Easter Island, Earth and the Future of Humanity.* Phoenix: Golden Phoenix Publishing, 2006.

Barclay, H.V. "Easter Island and Its Colossal Statues," *Rapa Nui Journal* vol. 23, no. 2, 2009: pp. 154–61.

Bellwood, P. *Man's Conquest of the Pacific.* Oxford: Oxford University Press, 1987.

Bennett Media Worldwide, *Mysteries of Easter Island,* 2009.

The Captain's Logbook: Easter Island/Rapa Nui 2003. Available online. URL: http://www.sergeking.com/Rapanui/index.html

The Chilling Tale of Easter Island. Available online. URL: www.unmeseum.org/easteri.htm

Cristino, Claudio P., and Patricia Vargas Casanova. "Ahu Tongariki, Easter Island: Chronological and Sociopolitical Significance," *Rapa Nui Journal* xiii/3, 1999: pp. 67–69.

D'Alleva, A. *Art and Artifacts of Polynesia.* Cambridge: Hurst Gallery, 1990.

Diamond, Jared. *Guns, Germs, and Steel: The Fates of Human Societies.* New York: W.W. Norton & Company, 1999.

———. *Collapse: How Societies Choose to Fail or Succeed.* New York: Viking, 2005.

Drake, Alan. *Easter Island: The Ceremonial Center of Orongo.* Los Osos, Calif.: Easter Island Foundation, 1992.

Easter Island Foundation. Available online. URL: http://islandheritage.org/wordpress/

Easter Island: Birdman Competition. Available online. URL: http://chile-travel.suite101.com/article.cfm/easter_island_birdman_competition

Easter Island: Moai Statues and Rock Art of Rapa Nui. Available online. URL: http://www.bradshawfoundation.com/easter/rock-art1.php

Easter Island Resources on the Internet Available online. URL: http://mysteriousplaces.com/Easter_Island/html/resources.html

"Easter Island: Statue Vandal Fined $17,000." *New York Times*, May 25, 2010.

Englert, F. Sebastián. *Island at the Center of the World*. New York: Charles Scribner's Sons, 1970.

First Inhabitants. Available online. URL: http://www.pbs.org/wgbh/nova/easter/civilization/first.html

The First New World Voyage of Christopher Columbus. Available online. URL: http://latinamericanhistory.about.com/od/latinamericatheconquest/p/Columbusfirst.htm

Fischer, Steven Roger. *Island at the End of the World: The Turbulent History of Easter Island*. London: Reaktion Books Ltd., 2005.

———. *Easter Island Studies: Contributions to the History of Rapanui in Memory of William T. Mulloy*. London: Oxbow Books, 1993.

Flenley, John, and Paul Bahn. *The Enigmas of Easter Island: Island on the Edge*. Oxford: Oxford University Press, 1992.

Heyerdahl, Thor. *Aku-Aku: The Secret of Easter Island*. New York: George Allen & Unwin Ltd., 1958.

———. *Fatu-Hiva: Back to Nature*. New York: Doubleday & Company, Inc., 1974.

———. *The RA Expeditions*. New York: Doubleday & Company, Inc., 1971.

Horley, Paul. "*Rongorongo* Tablet Keiti," *Rapa Nui Journal* vol. 24 (1) 2010: pp. 45–56.

Horley, Paul, and Georgia Lee. "Painted and Carved House Embellishments at Orongo Village, Easter Island," *Rapa Nui Journal* vol. 23 (2) 2009: pp. 106–124.

Howe, K.R., editor. *Vaka Moana Voyages of the Ancestors: The Discovery and Settlement of the Pacific*. Honolulu: University of Hawaii Press, 2009.

JWM Productions, *History—Digging for the Truth: Giants of Easter Island*, 2008.

Lee, Georgia. *Te Moana Nui: Exploring Lost Isles of the South Pacific*. Los Osos, Calif.: Easter Island Foundation, 2001.

———. *Rapa Nui, Island of Memory*. Los Osos, Calif.: Easter Island Foundation, 2006.

———. *An Uncommon Guide to Easter Island*. Arroyo Grande: International Resources, 1990.

———. *The Rock Art of Easter Island*. Los Angeles: UCLA Institute of Archaeology.

Lee, Georgia, and William Liller. "Easter Island's 'Sun Stones,' A Critique," *Journal of the Polynesian Society* 96(1) 1987: pp. 81–93.

Lewis, David, edited by Sir Derek Oulton. *We, the Navigators: The Ancient Art of Landfinding in the Pacific.* Honolulu: University of Hawaii Press, 1994.

McLaughlin, Shawn. *The Complete Guide to Easter Island.* Los Osos, Calif.: Easter Island Foundation, 2007.

Mieth, Andreas, and Hans-Rudolf Bork. *Easter Island—Rapa Nui: Scientific Pathways to Secrets of the Past.* Kiel, Germany: Department of Ecotechnology and Ecosystem Development, Ecology Center, Chrisstian-Albrechts-Universitä, 2004.

Mieth, Andreas. "Getting to Know You," *Rapa Nui Journal* vol. 24 (1) 2010: pp. 61–63.

Mulloy, W. *The Easter Island Bulletins of William Mulloy.* New York: World Monuments Fund and Easter Island Foundation, 1997.

Mulrooney, Mara A., Thegan N. Ladefoged, Christopher M. Stevenson, and Sonia Hooa. "The Myth of A.D. 1680: New Evidence From Hanga Hoʻonu, Rapa Nui (Easter Island)," *Rapa Nui Journal* vol. 23 (2) 2009: pp. 96–105.

Nainoa Thompson: In Search of History. Available online. URL: http://bosp.kcc.hawaii.edu/Horizons/horizons_1999/nainoa2.html

Parry, John H. *The Discovery of the Sea.* New York: Dial Press, 1974.

Pilot Productions, *Globe Trekker: Chile & Easter Island,* 2004.

Polynesian History & Origin: Wayfinders, a Pacific Odyssey. Available online. URL: http://www.pbs.org/wayfinders/polynesian8.html

Rapanui—The History of the Colonization of Easter Island. Available online. URL: http://www.about.com

Richards, Rhys. *Easter Island 1793 to 1861: Observations by Early Visitors Before the Slave Raids.* Los Osos, Calif.: Easter Island Foundation, 2008.

Rohter, Larry. "Easter Island Casino Plan Raises Fear of Cultural Erosion." *New York Times,* April 1, 2006.

Sacks, Oliver. *The Island of the Colorblind.* New York: Alfred A. Knopf, 1997.

Sharp, Andrew, editor. *The Journal of Jacob Roggeveen.* Oxford: Oxford University Press, 1970.

Stein, Rebecca L., and Philip L. Stein. *The Anthropology of Religion, Magic, and Witchcraft.* New York: Pearson, 2008.

Stone Giants. Available online. URL: http://www.pbs.org/wgbh/nova/easter/civilization/gaints.html

The Story of Easter Island. Available online. URL: http://mysteriousplaces.com/Easter_Island/html/tour2.html

Title House e-Distribution, *Easter Island: Eyes of the Moai,* 2001.

"Trans-Pacific Chicken." *New York Times,* June 9, 2007.

Vanderbes, Jennifer. *Easter Island: A Novel.* New York: Bantam Dell, 2003.

Vanderbes, Jennifer. "A Faraway Land Steeped in Mystery." *New York Times,* December 14, 2003.

Van Tilburg, Jo Anne. *Easter Island: Archaeology, Ecology, and Culture.* Washington D.C.: Smithsonian Institution Press, 1994.

———. *Among Stone Giants: The Life of Katherine Routledge and Her Remarkable Expedition to Easter Island.* New York: Scribner, 2003.

Von Däniken, Erich. *Chariots of the Gods.* New York: Berkley Publishing Group, 1969.

Wayfinders: A Pacific Odyssey Available online. URL: www.maidenvoyage.com/wayfindersdvd-info.html

Wilford, John Noble. "If These Stones Could Talk." *New York Times*, July 7, 1998.

Further Resources

Arnold, Caroline. *Easter Island: Giant Stone Statues Tell of a Rich and Tragic Past.* New York: Clarion Books, 2000.

Orliac, Catherine, and Michel Orliac. *Easter Island: Mystery of the Stone Giants.* New York: Harry N. Abrams, Inc., 1995.

Rapanui Press. *The Guide.* Rapa Nui, Chile. Rapa Nui Press, 1999.

Soza, Felipie L. *Easter Island: Rapa Nui.* Santiago, Chile: S&E S.A., 2007.

Web Sites

Easter Island
http://www.mysteriousplaces.com/Easter_Isld_Pge.html
This site gives the viewer a virtual tour of Easter Island, with an emphasis on beautiful photography of the moai.

Kon-Tiki Web Server
http://www.musemumsnett.no/kon-tiki/
Contains the scholarly papers from Norway's Kon-Tiki Museum, with a welcome from the famed explorer Thor Heyerdahl.

Polynesian Voyaging Society
http://leahi.kcc.hawaii.edu/org/pvs/
The Web site of the organization that investigates how the Polynesian seafarers discovered and settled the islands of the Pacific. Shows one what it is like to live for a month onboard a replica of an ancient voyaging canoe.

Rapanui
Http://www2.hawaii.edu/~ogden/piir/pacific/Rapanui.html
An excellent site for those eager to visit Easter Island.

Rap Nui Outrigger Club
http://www.netaxs.com/~trance/outrig.html
About the organization that gives young Rapanui people the opportunity to learn about their people's history while developing outrigger canoe paddling skills.

Sail of the Century: Hōkūle'a and the Voyage to Rapa Nui
http://archives.starbulletin.com/1999/06/07/hokulea/story1.html
How the celestial navigators embark on their most difficult, most important voyages of the last 25 years as they prepare to pass on their dreams to a second generation of voyagers. Contains Web camera to access images during the voyage.

Unofficial Easter Island Home Page
http://www.netaxes.com/~trance/rapanui.html
A wealth of information on Easter Island's history, culture, and tourism, with great additional Web links.

Picture Credits

Index

About the Author

RONALD A. REIS has written young adult biographies as well as books on the Dust Bowl, the Empire State Building, the New York City subway system, African Americans and the Civil War, and the World Trade Organization for Chelsea House. He is the technology department chair at Los Angeles Valley College.